COWBOY CULTURE

COWBOY CULTURE

CAPTURING THE SPIRIT OF THE OLD WEST
IN THE SIERRA NEVADA

SANDY POWELL

Skyhorse Publishing

Skyhorse Publishing books may be purchased in bulk at special discounts for sales promotion, corporate gifts, fund-raising, or educational purposes. Special editions can also be created to specifications. For details, contact the Special Sales Department, Skyhorse Publishing, 307 West 36th Street, 11th Floor, New York, NY 10018 or info@skyhorsepublishing.com.

Skyhorse® and Skyhorse Publishing® are registered trademarks of Skyhorse Publishing, Inc.®, a Delaware corporation.

Visit our website at www.skyhorsepublishing.com.

10 9 8 7 6 5 4 3 2 1

Library of Congress Cataloging-in-Publication Data is available on file.

Cover design by Mona Lin
Cover photo credit: Sandy Powell

Print ISBN: 978-1-5107-4226-0
Ebook ISBN: 978-1-5107-4227-7

Printed in China

Contents

INTRODUCTION

Some ask why I started this book project. Well, it started as an extension of my western photography but evolved into a present-day story of the Old West remaining in the California Sierra Nevada. The discovery of gold in the California Sierra Nevada was the driving force for the population explosion in the western states in the nineteenth century. There are many remnants in present-day California of the western migration from the mid-1800s: old mines, mining towns, old gravesites, wagon routes, stage routes, mountain men trails, and the Pony Express Trail.

Most Californians have little knowledge of California's great western history. They might have heard a blurb about the '49ers, but I bet that most can't even tell that story. The highways that cross the Sierra Nevada each have their own story—trails that were first used by the Indians were later explored by the mountain men, and later became routes for overland emigrants, stagecoach drivers, and Pony Express riders. Many men and women died en route to California while seeking a life with better opportunities. Their struggles, courage, and perseverance helped create the legacy of the American West.

The principal mission of this book is to document present-day western activities and preserve this western spirit for future generations. I also want to demonstrate that a fair amount of the Old West still endures today—passed down from previous generations and early settlers in the state. To help readers appreciate the difficult struggles of the early pioneers who blazed the trails to California, I have provided some historical context in the first few chapters to set a foundation for the book.

The Old West conjures up some romantic ideas from the bygone days, but the early pioneers who settled in the state faced much tragedy and despair while pursuing a better life. Their sacrifices should not be forgotten and should be celebrated. Many photos in this book capture this enduring spirit in present-day individuals—who still carry on the traditions either by working with their livestock or celebrating the early pioneers.

Driving down Highway 395, one is in awe of the Sierra Nevada dramatically jutting out of the ground and rising toward the sky like a large granite monument. But along the way, there are many hidden western activities happening in the background—moving cattle, pack mules being prepared for the upcoming season, and sheep being moved to the high country for summer grazing. Many of these ranchers and packers face tremendous obstacles with today's government bureaucracy but still continue with their hard work and dedication, carrying on with traditions passed on to them from previous generations. They are not doing it to become rich—they are doing it for the passion and a way of life that others can only envy from a distance.

When I spoke with Tim Erickson, a third-generation cattle rancher in the western Sierra, he shared with me a story about a conversation he had on an airplane recently. He was seated next to a woman who works in Washington, D.C. and he told her what he did for an occupation. She replied, "Really! There are still cowboys out there working cattle?" She thought it was from an era long ago and could not believe that people still raise cattle on the open range. Erickson shared his knowledge with her, hoping she would help others back East become more aware of this lifestyle. So I hope this book gets shared with her and others who have limited knowledge of the Old West that remains in the Sierra Nevada in this modern day and age.

Contrary to popular belief, very few miners "struck it rich" in the California's goldfields.

Photo Credit: Wikimedia, California Historical Society Collection.

CHAPTER ONE

THE DISCOVERY OF CALIFORNIA'S GOLD

On a cold morning in January in 1848, James Marshall was checking the tailrace of Sutter's sawmill, located on the American River, to see if it had been flushed of debris. He noticed small pieces of yellow metal shimmering in the water. All the workers dropped their tools to gather around Marshall to inspect his metal pieces. After testing it with his teeth, one of the workers exclaimed, "Gold, boys, gold!"

In 1848, the fate of the California territory would change overnight as Marshall discovered gold in the foothills of the Sierra Nevada. California's mighty treasure had finally been unlocked. The Indians had stumbled over it and ignored it for centuries. The Spanish and Mexicans, who had occupied the territory for almost 150 years, only saw California fit for the production of cowhides and wine. But that discovery in 1848 would change the history of California, and many parts of the West, forever.

The timing of the gold discovery was a bit uncanny since the United States was at war with Mexico and did not acquire the territory until a week later—February 2nd of 1848. The news frenzy did not make it back East until August of 1848, but the California Gold Rush was already set into motion.

Up to the year 1848, few Americans had made the journey to California—mountain men, fur trappers, ranchers, American military troops, and only a few adventurous emigrants. Most of the settlers had come by boat. Only the emigrants, mountain men, and some military battalions made the journey overland, by wagon or horseback. The California Trail was barely beaten down as a wagon trail, with the first wagons finding a passage across the Sierra Nevada in 1844 (see Wagon Drive chapter). But these trails across the Sierra Nevada would be expanded and developed as tens of thousands of emigrants made the perilous journey to California in 1849 and 1850 in covered wagons, with most finishing the journey with only the clothes on their back. But they were the lucky ones, as many emigrants and their livestock perished on the arduous journey through the Forty Mile Desert or crossing the Sierra Nevada. Those that did survive the insurmountable obstacles later learned that very few gold-seekers struck it rich.

Consequently, the gold rush hysteria boosted the population of this newly acquired US territory. Eighty thousand gold-seekers made the hazardous trip to California in the year of 1849—approximately 40,000 by boat and 40,000 by land.[1] The gold rush attracted a hardy and adventurous population to the state along with demands for other professions while spawning new industries. It brought experienced teamsters, innovative miners, new overland mail routes that used stagecoaches and mud wagons, mule packers, tradesmen, lawmen, cattle-ranchers, sheepherders, and farmers. These pioneers helped develop California's daring and enduring western spirit.

Many present-day Californians have little knowledge of California's great western history, with few only recalling the gold rush or the Donner Party. The highways that cross the Sierra Nevada each have their own story—they were once part of an Indian trail network that was later used by the mountain men who explored the Sierra, and later evolved into wagon and stagecoach roads. Many men and women perished trying to follow their dreams over these treacherous roads, which were not forgiving in their nature.

But it was a thrilling time during those early days when the wagon trains and stagecoaches raced to the California goldfields—on the trail where the dust and campfire smoke met. In the shadow

Thousands of wagons made the journey to California in 1849 and 1850. *Photo Credit: National Archives and Records.*

of the towering Sierra Nevada, the *real* Wild West—that Hollywood would spend a century trying to recreate—was born. And it still lives today, in the extraordinary people who pack mule strings into the mountains, race over mountain passes on horseback while recreating the Pony Express, and drive cattle out of the high country each fall. It lives on beneath the massive wheels of the twenty mule team wagons that roll through the sagebrush, and with the teamsters who command a team of six draft horses while pulling a historic wagon over a mountain pass.

I have been fortunate to meet some of these dedicated folks and capture them in photos. Many of these people gained their knowledge from previous generations while collecting stories along the way. The traditions and tales of the early pioneers have been passed down through many generations in the western community. Today

these traditions are celebrated at various western events, at the high-country pack stations, and on multi-generation cattle ranches.

I hope you enjoy the photo essay in the book. My goal was to capture and honor the spirit of the Old West that remains in the Sierra Nevada. It is not meant to be a history book, but there is a lot of western history that is relevant and worth sharing. If the book inspires you, then make a point to get out and enjoy our western history and celebrations. Take a mule-packing trip, visit an old mining town, enjoy some trail riding on horseback, go to Bishop Mule Days or the Draft Horse Classic, or cross one of the old wagon routes over the Sierra Nevada.

Happy Trails!

CALIFORNIA GOLD

The trail along which we now ride
Was made by folks with visions bold,
A westward moving human tide,
Who nurtured dreams of farms or gold.

From the promise of day's first light,
Through somber sand and sage, they rode
In savage heat and gelid night,
Bound for the distant Mother Lode.

Their deep grooved ruts are now obscure
Along the winding desert track
Where traveled once the pioneers
In some imagined days, way back.

For those who passed, the dreams are done;
And most who failed left tales untold
With wagon wheels and oxen bones
And wood crosses above their own.

In the debris of that vast land
Lay a pink bottle, half in sand,
Which sparkled in the twilight gold.
It held a faded note which told:

"Tis a helluva place where I have died.
I did not make it, but I'm glad I tried."

© David Drowley

This outrider is getting his horse ready for the
Lone Pine to Bishop Wagon Drive, with the
Eastern Sierra in the background.

Modern teamsters keep the western spirit alive in California today.

AN OVERVIEW OF THE SIERRA NEVADA

The Sierra Nevada is a four-hundred-mile mountain range that runs north-to-south and sits between the Central Valley of California and the Great Basin. The majority of the range lies in California, but a historically significant part lies in the state of Nevada. The northern end of the Sierra Nevada is bounded by the Susan River and Fredonyer Pass where it meets the Cascade Range; the southern boundary is the Tehachapi Pass. Each year, thousands of tourists visit the Sierra Nevada, making trips to Lake Tahoe, Yosemite National Park, Sequoia-Kings Canyon National Park, and the John Muir Trail—a well-known 210-mile trail that attracts backpackers from all over the world.

The elevation of the Sierra Nevada starts at 1,000 feet in the Central Valley, reaching a top elevation of 14,505 feet at the summit of Mount Whitney—the highest peak in the lower forty-eight states. With a major fault zone on the east side of the Sierra, the range started to uplift and tilt westward some four million years ago. This created a gentle westward slope and an abrupt, steep, east-facing slope. This gentle slope affects the weather patterns of the Sierra Nevada. A "rain shadow" is created as the moisture on the windward west side advances over the mountain slowly, sucking out all the moisture, leaving little precipitation on the leeward east side of the Sierra. As a result, much of the eastern side of the Sierra is a high desert.

The Sierra Nevada was first named on a map in 1776 by Pedro Font, who referred to the distant range of mountains as "una gran sierra nevada," translated to mean a great snow-covered mountain range. The literal translation is "snowy mountains"—Sierra (mountain range) and Nevada (snowy). While many people make reference to the Sierras or Sierra Nevadas, it is considered a redundant plural. Technically, the range should be referred to as the Sierra or Sierra Nevada.

The snowpack from the Sierra Nevada is a major source of water for the state of California and parts of northern Nevada. Snowfall is measured in feet, not inches, while accompanied with wind gusts

Working cowboys taking a break in the Eastern Sierra while moving cattle over the mountain.

up to 180 mph. In the 1850s, many of the pioneers who crossed the Sierra Nevada recorded residual snow on the Sierra passes measuring eight to twenty feet in the summer months in their journals. The Sierra Nevada is no stranger to big snowstorms—in winter months, the storms can be dangerous and tragic. Seven feet of snow can fall in a day. In the winter of 1906–1907, seventy-three feet of snow was recorded at Tamarack, California—a record that still stands today.[2]

These record snowfalls should not be forgotten when recalling the pioneers who had to cross the Sierra Nevada in the fall months—when the deadly snowstorms start to brew. The Donner Party learned the hard way, when many feet of snow fell overnight during their journey.

The Sierra Nevada is rich in western history but also diverse in topography, climate, and moisture resulting in diverse and complex eco-regions. These regions vary from scrub and chaparral zones, to montane forests, to subalpine forests and alpine meadows in the high country. The eastern side is commonly characterized with sagebrush, Pinyon pine, Jeffrey pine, and juniper at mid-elevations.

Map of the Sierra Nevada.

The western spirit is kept alive at various celebrations and events throughout the year. This is the Hangtown Christmas Parade in Placerville, California.

This California Rack Wagon is brought out for special events. The wagon was used to haul logs, fence posts, heavy sacks of grain, and other materials. In general, it was a good utility wagon on the farm a century ago.

Go West and Make Your Fortune — The Westwood Wagon Drive follows part of the Old Lassen Wagon Fork of the California Trail in the northern Sierra.

CHAPTER TWO

THE JOURNEY TO CALIFORNIA BY WAGON TRAIN

It is said that three thousand, two hundred wagons had passed the Fort before us, and three hundred more are now in the vicinity. We are surrounded by several large trains in full view.
—James Abbey, at Fort Kearny, Nebraska, 1850.

At the peak of the western migration in 1850, the sound of trace chains and creaking wagon wheels could be heard for hundreds of miles as thousands of wagons made the journey to California. Since the end of colonial times, American pioneers have always had a tendency to move west. As land treaties opened up the lands in the West, the western frontier became this vast, undeveloped land of opportunity—offering promises of a new life.

But the discovery of gold at Sutter's Mill in California in 1848 opened the floodgates as thousands of emigrants followed the wave of a new life and instant wealth. Who could be held back from the luring promise of free gold, free land, and adventure! Many uprooted their former lives, bought a wagon and the necessary provisions, and joined an emigrant wagon train. A limited number of wagons had successfully made the overland trip to Oregon in the early 1840s, establishing the Oregon Trail, but wagon routes to California were not clearly defined. The new frontier started at the Missouri River, where civilization came to an abrupt halt. This was no ordinary wagon journey—this overland trip was 2,000 to 2,400 miles in length, taking four to six months to complete, and would later become known as the California Trail.

For those who have never seen a wagon train, it was no small feat to get a wagon outfit together, especially for a cross-country trip. Imagine having to sell most of your worldly possessions, then fit 1,500 to 2,000 pounds of provisions into a wagon to survive the four- to six-month journey. Remember, there were no Starbucks or 7-Elevens along the way. There was not a clearly marked route once you passed through Salt Lake City, and in some parts there was no real trail. To make matters worse, there were no fully explored maps. The directions were mostly word of mouth—passed down from the mountain men and fur traders who had explored the territory. Also, few from the East had an understanding of deserts and tall snow-covered mountains.

Furthermore, the overland travelers had to be totally self-reliant. For today's younger generation that has grown up with the internet and cellphones, this cannot be emphasized enough. If you encountered a broken wheel, you had to fix it en route. If people in your party or your animals got sick, you had to figure out a remedy—a serious concern since cholera was quite prevalent along the first half of the route. And there was absolutely no communication with the outside world; there were only the folks in your wagon train. But there was one saving grace. Along the route, there were a few government "fort" outposts that offered some limited supplies for restocking. But the forts were few in number, so your food supply was a finite resource for the trip, requiring you to hunt along the route to supplement your supplies.

Equally important was finding forage for the animals. Once the emigrants entered the Utah and Nevada regions, there was very limited grass and forage; plus, they were competing with other wagons en route for animal forage. It was an unforgiving territory. Much

Oregon Trail

California Trail

Fort Hall

Oregon-California Trail

Salt Lake City

St. Joseph

Sutter's Fort

Sacramento

Death Valley 49ers Route

Independence

Los Angeles

of the water in the Great Basin area was alkaline, so travellers had to haul their water in barrels. Add to those challenges that the heat was intense, there were deep sand crossings, and there was a lack of shade. It is doubtful that many people in today's society could find the courage, perseverance, and know-how to accomplish such a trip. Ultimately, these brave souls faced physical and emotional challenges, failure, and extreme suffering on their journey.

Many wagon trains bound for California in 1849 and 1850 relied on a guidebook written by Lansford Hastings—*The Emigrant's Guide to Oregon and California in 1845*. This guide was more of an inflated sales brochure rather than a guidebook offering pertinent advice to reach this distant, foreign land. Hastings wrote about California having a perpetual spring, immense herds of animals, heavy timber stands, and bountiful fisheries. Only 20 percent of the book explained "how to travel" to California, while Hastings exaggerated about the relative ease of getting wagons from Fort Hall to San Francisco—making it sound like a sightseeing trip. Nothing could be further from the truth. The second half of the trip was the most excruciating—many emigrants and livestock perished in what became known as the *Forty Mile Desert* of Nevada.

As they crossed the desert, their prized possessions became meaningless. Fine China, silver, furniture, mattresses, and mining tools were abandoned along the trail to lighten their load. Few had prepared for this "hell hole of a desert" and were not equipped with enough food and water to cross the desert.[3]

Morning comes…and presents a scene more horrid than the route of a defeated army; dead stock line the road; wagons, rifles, tents, clothes, everything but food may be found scattered along the road…men scattered along the plain and stretched out among the dead stock like corpses, fills out the picture.—Eleazer Stillman Ingalls en route to California, 1850.

HISTORY OF EMIGRANT WAGON TRAINS TO CALIFORNIA

If there were no roads or trails to California crossing the Sierra Nevada, how did the early emigrants find a way through this

Opposite: Map of Overland Trails.
National Map Courtesy of U.S. Geological Survey, Department of the Interior.

Wagons crossing the Owens River in the Eastern Sierra.

Sunrise is a glorious time on the wagon drives.

Above: The emigrants actually walked much of the route to help keep the load lighter for the animals. The wagon train would travel an average of two miles per hour for the 2000-mile journey. *Used by permission, Utah State Historical Society.*

unknown territory? There were Americans already settled in the Central Valley and coastal regions of California who came by boat or on the precarious Old Spanish Trail—a longer, southern route that was better suited for pack animals before 1850. Before 1848, California was known as "Alta California" and was part of the Mexican territory. A few Americans had received provisional Spanish land grants for ranching and settled in Alta California.

An important distinction about these overland travelers, as compared to the mountain men and earlier settlers, is that the emigrants (also called Emigrant Societies) were made up of families and single men who chose to travel by wagon—not pack animals. Gold had not been discovered yet, so that was not their motivation. Leaving behind a life of uncertainty, they came to Oregon and California seeking adventure and new opportunities. They first followed the established Oregon Trail, then splintered off the trail in Idaho to find a new route to California, which required crossing the Sierra Nevada.

These brave pioneers tested the various crossings over the treacherous Sierra Nevada, hoping to find the easiest route. But it should be pointed out that the Sierra Nevada can be dangerous and deadly with its unpredictable snowstorms. In winter months, seven feet of snow can fall in a day and snowfall is not unusual in the summer and early fall months. So wagon travel during the winter months was prohibitive and needed to be completed before the cold fall months. To complicate matters, there was eight to twenty feet of snow (recorded in journals from the 1850s) on many of the passes in the summer, leftover from the previous winter.

Most people recall the ill-fated Donner party trying to cross the Sierra in 1846, but few have heard about the heroic efforts of the Bidwell-Bartleson party. In 1841, the Bidwell-Bartleson party was the first emigrant party to cross the Sierra Nevada through the perilous Sonora Pass region. Trying to find a route to California,

Left: The wagon circle at nighttime. On the wagon trains migrating to the West, the wagon circles contained the livestock so they wouldn't stray at night, while the pioneers slept on the outside of the circle. Indian attacks did not occur in the earlier years of the westward migration, with the Indians more interested in stealing livestock than killing emigrants.

they used the letters of Dr. John Marsh that were printed in the Missouri newspapers as a guide. Marsh had traveled to California in 1836 and provided some information about the Oregon Trail and some notes about finding the Humboldt River (also known as the St. Mary's River) in northern Nevada, but he offered no advice about how to cross the Sierra Nevada. Compounding their problems, they were a party of "green recruits"—none had ever traveled west of the Missouri River.[4]

Luck was on their side when they were able to hook up with another party that had hired Thomas Fitzpatrick, a notable mountain man, to guide them toward Oregon. Before reaching Fort Hall in Idaho, their party split toward California. They had to overcome many challenges in the region that would become the Utah Territory. In early September, they had trouble finding the head of the Humboldt River. It was getting late in the season, so the cold weather and the grueling journey was taking its toll on their animals. The wagons were becoming a liability, so they abandoned them, in what is now northern Nevada. They used their horses and mules as pack animals to cross the Forty Mile Desert and to climb over the Sierra Nevada near Sonora Pass before almost starving to death. Armed with courage and youth, the party became the first American overland emigrants to cross the Sierra Nevada and enter California.

Because the Bidwell-Bartleson party failed to find a viable route for future wagon travel, no one followed in their path. However, their journey should not be discounted. Today, Sonora Pass (Highway 108) is still a difficult route to navigate in an automobile. The daunting pass is 9,623 feet in elevation and closed in the winter. Because of the many hairpin-turns and 26 percent grade, semi-trucks and longer trailers are prohibited on the highway. Consequently, other routes were explored by the pioneers in the upcoming years.

In 1844, the Stephens-Townsend-Murphy party was officially the first wagon train to cross the Sierra Nevada, forging a new route near Donner Pass. The group of ten families could not have made the difficult journey without the help of mountain men—Caleb Greenwood and Isaac Hitchcock.[5] The group of emigrants made the journey with no casualties—but this was mostly due to good leadership, some luck, and enough food provisions to get them through the desert and over the Sierra Nevada.

"This is the same land, through
    Which the pioneers led –
This is the same relentless region
    From which the homesteaders fled…
These are the same stars that many
    Before have upon gazed.
These are the same beaten-down valleys
    Where livestock tried to graze."

—Sallie Knowles Joseph

When they started their overland journey, only two wagon trains had successfully made it to California (after abandoning their wagons en route), and no information had been sent back for future overland travelers. After leaving the headwaters of the Humboldt River, the Stephens-Townsend-Murphy party was unsure of the route. With a bit of luck on their side, they consulted a Paiute Indian Chief through sign language, whom they named Truckee (through their interpretations). The Indian guided them through the Forty Mile Desert to find an easterly river, which was later named after the Indian guide—the Truckee River. This route became the northern "Truckee" route of the Forty Mile Desert crossing. This life-saving information led the party to the next step of their journey—crossing the Sierra Nevada up the precipitous route near Donner Lake.

Before reaching the lake, the party divided up, with part of the group heading south on horseback and eventually finding a route over the Sierra around Lake Tahoe to Sutter's Fort. The remaining party abandoned six wagons and took the five remaining wagons up the difficult terrain. They had to travel through two feet of snow and pull their wagons up over a ten-foot rock ledge with chains.[6]

They finally crossed the Sierra Nevada on November 25, 1844, and made it to the Yuba River valley. There they camped and waited out the heavy winter storms. In mid-winter, a rescue party from Sutter's Fort trekked through deep snow to help save the survivors. Despite the Donner Pass area being one of the snowiest regions in the world, the entire party survived the trip with their courage and fortitude.

Not all wagon trains were so fortunate.

After the successful '44 overland crossing, the trail became more beaten down, and new end-routes were added or relocated in the coming years, to become known as the "California Trail." But in 1846, known as the year of the Donner Party, the fate of this wagon party would become a menacing shadow for future wagon trains. That year the party encountered several mishaps, but the worst one was following the shortcut promoted by the unscrupulous Lansford Hastings.

Hastings was traveling eastward in hopes of promoting his new shortcut (later named the Hastings Cutoff) through the Wasatch Mountains, which was said to shorten the journey by hundreds of miles. Hastings only explored part of the route on horseback and did not consider the obstacles the route presented to wagon trains.

It was a reckless decision made by the Donner Party to follow this goose-chase through the Wasatch Mountains while losing approximately three weeks of travel time. This so-called shortcut required scouting out a feasible route for the wagons and cutting a new trail. Some canyons were so narrow that their wagons barely fit between the canyon walls and the river. Over the course of twenty-one days, they had only traveled thirty-six miles.

Exhausted, short on supplies, and demoralized, the group finally crossed the desert and approached their final leg of the journey—the Sierra Nevada. The party didn't start to cross the Sierra Nevada until mid-October and got caught in a terrible snowstorm. "A Sierran storm was unknown to them…[it] lasted eight days… the snow lay eight feet deep…twenty-five days of suffering and starvation… the necessity of cannibalism pressing closer."[7] Surprisingly, forty-eight

Forty Mile Desert Map.

"Striations form with earthly colors,
Preserving history, layer upon layer to view…
And heat waves dance along the wagon tracks,
Making the distant mirages come true."

—Sallie Knowles Joseph

members survived the brutal ordeal and the story would be etched in California's history forever.

Also occurring in 1846, the United States had territorial disputes with Mexico in Texas which resulted in a declaration of war. This Mexican-American war involved Alta California (part of the Mexican territory), where some select Americans had previously received provisional Spanish land grants for ranching. The Treaty of Guadalupe Hidalgo formally ended the war in 1848, just as gold was being discovered in Northern California, with the United States gaining ownership of California, New Mexico, Arizona, Nevada, Texas, and Utah.

On January 24, 1848, the greatest event to affect the outcome of the California Trail occurred. "Some kind of metal that looks like gold" was found at Sutter's Mill and the news did not reach the eastern United States until August of 1848. So 1849 ushered in the first year of the "gold rush" to California. The gold fever attracted many greenhorns—city folks who knew nothing of camping nor one end of an ox or mule from the other.

None could predict how large "the great California caravan" would be nor the effects of it on water and forage along the route. At Fort Kearny in June of 1849, over 5500 wagons were counted, providing an approximate size of the migration.[8] Three major end-routes were utilized, helping to spread out the wagons: the Lassen trail, the Truckee trail, and the Carson trail.

This huge migration of people and wagons had dire consequences for many since water and grass were scarce in the latter half of the journey. It was estimated that half the wagons were abandoned on this part of the journey, along with useless property that was hauled along, leaving these emigrants to walk a good portion of the trail to succeed.

After the disastrous journey of the Donner Party in 1846, many wagon trains recalled their saga when making decisions about crossing the Sierra Nevada late in the season. In 1849, approximately one hundred wagons ended up outside of Salt Lake City too late in the season to make the hazardous journey over the Sierra Nevada range. Not wanting to wait out the winter in Salt Lake City, they decided to follow the Old Spanish Trail—which bypassed the northern Sierra Nevada—allowing them to travel later in the season. The Old Spanish Trail was known as the "most arduous and crookedest" trail in the West, while it added hundreds of miles to the

This historic Weber wagon, circa 1910, is participating in a present-day wagon drive. The Weber Wagon Company was founded in the mid-1800s and they had a solid reputation for their quality wagons.

journey to California. Additionally, the route did not provide much grazing and there was a lack of water over stretches of the trail. Some said the trail was only fit for pack animals.

Shortly after starting their journey, they met some men on horseback who were carrying a hand-drawn map that showed an unexplored shortcut through the desert, shaving almost five hundred miles off the journey. But this shortcut would have dire consequences for the group of pioneers.

Many turned back after confronting nearly impassable sections, leaving about twenty wagons (which ended up in present-day Death Valley) thinking they only had one more mountain range to cross, when in fact there were five more mountain ranges to be crossed. Because women and children were a burden on the speed of a wagon train, the group splintered into smaller factions with many differing opinions on the best route to follow. While stuck in this desolate, forbidding valley of salt and sand, their food supplies became exhausted and their oxen were dying of starvation. So

William Lewis Manley and John Rogers walked 250 miles on foot, one way, to scout for an evacuation route. After two weeks they found some civilization in the present-day Santa Clarita area.

Eventually, they returned with food, horses, and the famous one-eyed mule for the remaining survivors. During their return trip, the horses died because they couldn't live off the brush nor tolerate the alkaline water. The one-eyed mule not only survived the journey but performed acrobatic feats along the cliffs in a canyon in the Panamint Mountains.

The children were sick from malnourishment, one of the women was quietly pregnant, and the oxen were suffering, but the group miraculously made the harrowing journey out, moving ever so slowly. Upon leaving, one woman turned back to the valley and said "Goodbye Death Valley," and the name stuck. They eventually crossed the southern Sierra Nevada and reached civilization in March of 1850. This group of heroic survivors would later be called the "Death Valley '49ers." To demonstrate the toll of the death-defying trip, one of the men was a healthy 180 pounds when he started the trip and weighed only eighty pounds when he finished the journey.

Regardless of the route chosen, the last half of the journey to California was a grueling test of endurance, testing the pioneers with a multitude of hardships. The journals from the great migration of 1849 and 1850 should serve as a grim reminder of their harrowing journey for future generations:

In 1850, Carlisle Abbott made the journey to California and spoke about the problems with cholera in the Platte Valley. He shared, "The next trouble we had was with cholera. It struck the tide of emigration like a cyclone, and on both sides of the Platte. The dates on the little headboards along the road were from one to three days old."[9]

Abbott also spoke of the agony traveling through the Forty Mile Desert. "The last fifteen miles, however, was an almost unbroken stretch of billows of sand, in which a horse's hoof would sink and be covered at every step, and at a point about five miles out in this sand…was a spot then known as Destruction Flat. Numerous buzzards had been sailing along behind us, watching and waiting for man or beast to fall…there were loose horses and oxen wandering listlessly

"At the mercy of the wind, like a cloud in the sky,
Along the mystical trail of tumbleweeds...
Ridin' easy, my friend, with old memories behind,
Without question, we go where destiny leads."

—Sallie Knowles Joseph

about in an endeavor to escape the fierce heat that beat down as if coming from a furnace."

On a different wagon train in 1850, James Abbey recorded in his journal: "The desert through which we are passing is strewed with dead cattle, mules, and horses. I counted in a distance of fifteen miles—three hundred fifty dead horses, two hundred eighty oxen, and one hundred twenty mules; and hundreds of others are left behind being unable to keep up. Such is traveling through the desert. These dead animals, decaying on the road, keep the air scented all the way through."[10]

After crossing the Forty Mile Desert, James Abbey and his party started the ascent to Carson Pass, elevation 8,574 feet, in the Sierra Nevada. Abbey shares some of their challenges of maneuvering their wagons on the climb: "Of all the rough roads I have ever seen or

even imagined, this beats them. Rocks from the size of a flour barrel to that of a meeting house are strewed all along the road, and these we are compelled to clamber and squeeze our [wagons] through as best we can."[11]

After getting through Hope Valley, they started the final climb. Abbey notes, "This summit is covered with snow to the depth of eight feet...freezing as it would on a December day at home. It was determined to throw one of our wagons away and double team." After traveling a half-mile, the oxen still struggled to pull the wagons on the steep ascent. So they abandoned their wagons, packed some provisions on their oxen, and finished the final climb. They successfully made it to the goldfields by late August but, as he learned along with many other prospectors, very few who made this daring and arduous journey "struck it rich."[12]

The wagon trains that made the overland journey to California were more than a group of wagons en route to the goldfields. These brave pioneers had to overcome dangerous river crossings, Indian attacks, disease, starvation, dehydration, severe heat, snowstorms, and the unexpected. It was estimated that 20,000 emigrants lost their lives on the California Trail.[13] Over time, these wagon trains became a symbol of the western expansion to California—a symbol representing the enduring human spirit that overcame numerous obstacles in spite of extreme hardship.

Westward Ho!

Wagons enter Desolation Canyon on the Death Valley Wagon Drive. Even though the modern-day Death Valley Wagon Train does not cross the Sierra, it honors the pioneers who got lost in Death Valley and eventually crossed the southern Sierra Nevada.

Opposite, top left: Some years, the Death Valley Wagon drive has to contend with some water crossings since Death Valley receives its only precipitation in the winter.

Opposite, top right: Some wagon drives pass historic relics from the mining days. This outrider passes an old lime kiln. The lime was used in the cyanide processing of gold and silver ores.

Opposite, bottom left: The Old West Trio entertains the Death Valley '49ers Encampment and wagon drive participants.

Opposite, bottom right: An outrider accompanies the wagon drive; the outrider usually rides along with a wagon and teamster. The role of the outrider is to be on-call for the teamster for any problems that might arise on the trail. The outriders are also the primary communication between the wagon master and other teamsters.

Right: Entering Badwater Basin in Death Valley, which has the lowest point in North America, with an elevation of 282 feet below sea level.

MODERN DAY WAGON DRIVES

As a way to honor these early pioneers, there are current-day wagon drives that follow sections of these old wagon routes. Stepping back in time, these modern pioneers experience living in the past with only a few modern conveniences. Some of the recent wagon drives in the Sierra Nevada have included: the Highway 50 Wagon Train, the Sonora Pass Wagon Train, the Sesquicentennial Wagon Drive, the Death Valley Wagon Train, the Lone Pine to Bishop Wagon Drive, Days of 49 Wagon Train, the Henness Pass Wagon Drive, the Pahrump Wagon Drive, and the Westwood Wagon Drive.

In northern Nevada, the Fearful Crossing Wagon Drive organized by Bill Adams, covers the agonizing desert section between the Humboldt Sink and Carson Valley—known as The Forty Mile Desert. Even with all the modern comforts, water trucks (for the animals), and food provided for the humans and animals, the Forty Mile Desert can still be a hard trip. Mike and Nancy Kerson, from Northern California, have participated in this drive three times, as outriders on their horses, and reminisced about some of the hardships along the drive.

Nancy Kerson shared: "One year a woman succumbed to heat exhaustion and needed attention. Mike went back to help while the rest of us continued. We were in that crunchy alkali part of the desert when I realized that I was by myself. I came to this water crossing… but I hesitate to call it water. It looked like poison because it was black, green, and yellow in color. So I retreated and went to look for the Highway 95 Bridge Crossing—recalling that the pioneers would have had to wade through it while trying to prevent their thirsty stock from drinking the poisonous water. At this location, the pioneers would have gone a day or two without water.

"Another time we were with a desert-savvy couple who saw this thick brown line on the horizon. The woman said that it was a sandstorm and it would arrive within an hour. It hit us like a wall of pelting sand and wouldn't let up for hours. Even with bandanas and sunglasses, it felt like sandpaper. Visibility varied from near blackout to being able to make out shapes several feet ahead. In camp, high winds prevented us from setting up tents until after dark. That particular night was supposed to be our big BBQ celebration, but cooking in the high winds was a challenge. The cooking team was finally able to make some dinner, which included generous helpings of sand! Even so, we had to remind ourselves that our conditions would have been considered 'glamping' compared to the early emigrant travelers," Kerson concluded.

I have had the opportunity to participate in several wagon drives to gain firsthand knowledge of wagon travel. I learned that these present-day drives are cushy vacations compared to pioneer travel. I asked some of the teamsters why they do these drives year-after-year and Ron Remy of Leona Valley, California summed it up nicely. "We are trying to keep the spirit of the pioneers alive. You don't understand the hardships of the pioneers until you do one of these drives. In comparison, we have all the modern conveniences which make their journey even more appreciated—we have queen-size mattresses, ice chests, porta-potties, pre-cooked meals, gas stoves, graded dirt roads, over-stuffed seats, and pneumatic tires."

Nolan Darnell, wagon master for the Westwood Drive, leads the wagons through the green forests and lush meadows in the Northern Sierra. The drive follows parts of the Lassen fork of the California Trail.

Nolan Darnell, a long-time teamster in Northern California, also shared, "As we move further away from the horse-drawn era, wagon trains are something from our past that need to be kept alive, so we have an understanding and appreciation of what it required to cross America by wagon in the 1800s. These modern-day drives give you a taste of what it was like and how tough our ancestors had to be to make the cross-country trip."

Today there is an annual wagon drive that commemorates the spirit of the unwilling discoverers of Death Valley, who eventually crossed the southern Sierra Nevada. The annual Corral 14 Death Valley Wagon Train was started in 1967 and each year retraces the '49ers steps through Death Valley National Park in November. The club follows either a one hundred mile/ten day route or a sixty mile/ six day route, with there being no cell service or contact with the outside world for most of the drive.

With the long history of the club's drive, there are many stories collected over the years. Broken wheels, forgotten neck-yokes, sick or exhausted animals, and a runaway team are not uncommon along this journey. Loose animals at night are par for the course, but the runaway mule story is still savored and shared…to remind everyone of the hazards in the desert.

Norm Noftsier, a former wagon master for the Death Valley drive, recalls the story: "A team of mules, owned by Bob Cleveland, got loose one night. Everyone went out searching for a good three hours with no luck. The next morning they tracked the mules for a few miles but lost their trail. And there was

Most of the wagons on these modern drives are equipped with pneumatic tires (for comfort), but a few of the historical wagons also join the drives.

Wagon repairs and shoeing horses are common on wagon drives. Just like the pioneers, the teamsters have to be self-reliant.

even a helicopter that took a quick look around from above. Three days later the mules just showed up in camp with an unapologetic look—like it was no big deal." This story truly demonstrates the resilience of the mule in the desert.

Shannon Alcott, whose husband grew up on the wagon drive as a kid, shared her fears about participating in the drive for the first time. "As a horse person, I was intrigued. However, the idea of no wifi, no civilization, and being stuck in a wagon for a week was a bit overwhelming. My fears were soon put to ease when I realized what an incredible experience it was to retrace the '49ers steps in this spectacular setting. But I also recognized the drive was the foundation for my husband's upbringing. We are now introducing our kids, who will be the next generation on this historic wagon drive," Alcott shared.

Wagons Ho!

Top: The wagon drive participants must be prepared for all types of weather in the Sierra Nevada. It briefly snowed on this drive in the month of May.

Bottom: After a day on the trail, the animals love to roll around in the dirt at the end of the day.

Wagon Trails

They left their father's hearths, those stalwart pioneers,
To follow their dreams to the West seeking new frontiers.
They laded Conestoga wagons and without a backward glance,
With faith and fortitude, ventured into that vast expanse!

They gathered at Independence to form a wagon train,
Then, ferried the Mighty Mo to trek the featureless plain.
They followed the rutted California Trail of those who'd gone before,
Never sensing the hazards and trials that were to be in store!

They were met with savages, mud, dust and howling gales,
Trudging westward, ever westward over endless hills and vales.
With visions of virgin homestead land they followed the sun.
They wouldn't be deterred from the migration they had begun!

"Prairie schooners" were crammed with goods and vital tools,
And were drawn by plodding oxen and cantankerous mules.
The caravan was under the command of a crusty wagon master.
Not to obey his ever bidding was sure to court disaster!

Alas, they left many desolate graves along the rutted track,
Victims of exhaustion, disease and fearful Indian attack.
They conquered interminable valleys and towering crests,
To fulfill their aspirations and complete their western quests!

© Robert L. Hinshaw

Background: A wagon train accompanies the Reno
Rodeo Cattle Drive in the Eastern Sierra.

The *Days of '49 Wagon Train*, hosted by the Kit Carson Mountain Men, travel through the Gold Country in the foothills of the Sierra celebrating California's pioneer heritage.

On the *Days of '49 Wagon Train*, the wagons pass an old stone foundation (right side of photo) that was a stage stop in the 1800s—near Drytown, California.

The outriders and teamsters enjoy the beautiful countryside on the *Days of '49 Wagon Train*, in the month of April.

THE HIGHWAY 50 WAGON TRAIN

Traveling in a wagon train for eight days following an old western migration route provides some valuable insight into the past, which is much more fun than reading about it in a history book. California is rich in western history and there is a multitude of routes that emigrants took to cross the Sierra Nevada by wagon. As more wagons made the trip to California, some passes became easier to navigate than others. One of the more popular routes was the Highway 50 route, known as the *Roaring Road* in the 1850s. It was so crowded that wagons could be backed up for a day or two in the peak months.

Two freight wagons pulled by a ten-mule hitch with a teamster riding a wheeler and controlling the team with a jerk line. *Photo courtesy of the Highway 50 Wagon Train Association. Circa, 1967.*

The Highway 50 Wagon Train has been celebrating this wagon route for seventy years. It started in 1949, coinciding with the one hundredth anniversary of the forty-niners and the Gold Rush. The original intentions of the Highway 50 Wagon Train were to emulate a freight wagon train crossing the *Roaring Road* in the 1800s—with participants dressed in appropriate period-piece clothing. Since the highway is a major route for Lake Tahoe traffic, the wagon train has the California Highway Patrol escort them throughout the route.

The Highway 50 Wagon Train Association owns two original freight wagons that were used on the *Roaring Road* route in the 1800s. One weighs 3,200 pounds, the other approximately 2,500 pounds. Some years they are hooked together and pulled by eight to ten horses or mules. Over the years, it has gotten harder and harder to find proficient teamsters who can drive an eight-horse hitch or a ten-horse hitch, let alone navigate the team over mountain passes. These teamsters are a dying breed. Because of this, most years the wagons are pulled separately by a six-and a four-horse hitch.

I've always been curious how a teamster manages an eight-horse hitch on the mountain passes. Rick Newborn, one of the teamsters who has driven the eight-horse-hitch numerous times, explained the technique to me. He shared, "You are basically driving four teams, and there are a couple of ways to do it. I first learned using all eight lines, four reins in each hand. It is really hard on your hands, and you have to get your hands in shape because they will ultimately cramp really bad. It is actually harder to work the team on the downhill. You have to manage the power of the team. On the downhill, you are only using the power of the "wheelers" (rear horses) to provide the horse braking power, as they hold back the wagon. To keep everything stretched out and taut, you also have to manage your lead horses, keeping them moving at just the right pace. And you also have the brakeman working the brakes to keep the weight off the horses. There is a lot of finessing to get all the components just right.

"On the uphill, the power is distributed more evenly, with all eight horses pulling their share. So you can see why the wheelers are the most important team since they are providing power on the uphill and the downhill. And this is why the wheelers are the tallest, heaviest, and strongest of the teams."

The wagon train coming around the bend on Echo Summit, with Lake Tahoe in the background.

Driving an eight-horse hitch requires a tremendous amount of skill, in addition to the brute strength and stamina needed to manage the reins for eight hours at a time. The driver has to hold thirty to forty pounds of reins, but once the horses exert some pressure, that can equate to seventy-five pounds of pressure. Newborn also shared that driving a "show hitch" is very different since the driver might only be in the show ring for twenty to thirty minutes on flat ground, as compared to eight or more hours in the mountains.

There have been numerous starting points in Nevada for the wagon train—Zephyr Cove, Round Hill, and Dayton—but the route always ends in Placerville, California, making it a bi-state journey. And every imaginable type of weather has been encountered over the years, from blistering heat to blizzards, in the early summer months. Since the route crosses Echo Summit, at an elevation of 7,382 feet, the threat of a snowstorm should not be discounted. In the early 1990s, Oliver Millhouse was driving the eight-horse hitch when a blizzard hit the Sierra Nevada. It was snowing so hard that Millhouse could not see his "leaders" in the front. To make matters worse, it was almost impossible for him to hold onto the eight horses with frozen hands. The storm lasted a day and somehow the steadfast Millhouse persevered.

In its glory days, the wagon train had up to thirty wagons participate on the drive, along with one hundred fifty to two hundred outriders. The wagon train would be over a mile long. I'm sure a lot of tourists slammed on their brakes in amazement when they came around the corner and saw a mile-long western caravan of wagons. Today the wagon train has about ten to fifteen wagons participating annually. Many challenges remain for the wagon train going forward. It is becoming more difficult to find stopovers and campsites along the route since land parcels get sold and developed on a regular basis.

There have been many stories and memories collected over the years for this historic wagon train. One year Queen Elizabeth was visiting California and the state diplomats lined up an itinerary for her. But she was quite interested in seeing some of the Old West and requested a visit with the Highway 50 Wagon Train. Since the Queen travels with her Guard, precautions would have to be taken. That particular year, the Kit Carson Mountain Men were escorting the wagon train, and this lively group is notorious for their colorful language and antique weapon collection. The Queen's Guard had to pre-check the group for weapons, with the mountain men averaging thirteen weapons each—including pistols, rifles, and knives. The Guard was

Traveling along on old wagon route that crosses the Sierra Nevada, the Highway 50 Wagon Train has been celebrating this route for over seventy years.

astonished when they checked in about two hundred weapons—I think they got an arousing dose of the Old West that day.

The week-long trip is filled with BBQs, storytelling, and some western celebrations along the route, ending with a parade in Placerville. Jill Carr recalls when she saw her first Highway 50 Wagon Train come through Placerville in 1963. As a 10-year-old child, the wagon train made an indelible impression on her, a memory she has cherished throughout her lifetime. "I'll never forget the goosebumps and thrill I experienced when I first saw the lead hitch with so many horses. As they passed by me, I felt the ground shake from the large draft horses and wagon wheels," Carr says.

As an adult, Carr acquired a horse and a buckboard wagon and participated in her first wagon drive in 1989. Today she is one of the few qualified brakemen/women that are specially trained to help operate the brakes on the large freight wagon.

Throughout the seventy-year history of the drive, many generations of families have participated on the Highway 50 Wagon Train. Dianna Newborn was the first woman to command the role of the wagon master in 2001—a big honor for Newborn, who was following in her grandparents' footsteps. They were part of the original group that founded the wagon train. Today, Crystal Newborn, daughter of Dianna and Rick Newborn, has taken over the reins of the wagon train. Crystal was 24 years old in 2017 when she became the youngest wagon master for the group. With Crystal managing the role in the upcoming years, she is providing the foundation for the next generation.

Long Live the Wagon Train!

A six-horse hitch pulls one of the freight wagons up Echo Summit, elevation 7,382 feet.

Stagecoaches helped keep California connected to the rest of the country during the 1850s by moving mail and important news through the frontier in a timely manner.

CHAPTER THREE

THE OVERLAND MAIL – THE ROLE OF THE STAGECOACH IN THE WESTERN EXPANSION

The history of the overland mail is a misunderstood story about expediting mail to California through the western frontier shortly after the discovery of gold. Without the overland mail companies, the West would not have been graced with stories about the heroic efforts of stagecoach drivers braving treacherous terrain, Indian attacks, and the infamous highwaymen. In the 1800s, the stagecoaches were seen to be glamorous, providing travel to far-away places. Hollywood embraced the stereotypical characters and visual stories of stagecoaches—embellishing the robberies and hold-ups while transporting the newcomers and city folks to the new outposts in the West.

In many films, the stagecoach is pulled by a fast and fierce team of horses. The most well-known overland mail company—the Butterfield Overland Mail Company—was known for using mustangs and unbroken mules which could sometimes provide unruly speed. From one of the episodes in the *Stagecoach West* television series, a customer asks if the stage conductor is the driver in which he replies, "it takes a steadier hand than mine to handle a six-up of them fiery-eyed sons of satans!"[15]

One of the most memorable Hollywood stagecoach scenes occurred in John Ford's 1939 film, *Stagecoach*. The legendary stuntman Yakima Canutt will always be remembered for his famous performance in *Stagecoach*—leaping from a galloping horse onto the stagecoach's lead horse (of a six-horse hitch), then slipping between the lead horses, and falling under the horses and coach, all at a full-paced gallop. This performance is probably the most dangerous stunt ever attempted — EVER!

"A stagecoach is like a can of sardines, there is always room for just one more."[14] *Photo courtesy of California State University, Chico, Meriam Library Special Collections.*

But in reality, the Hollywood depiction does not quite match up with real-life history. The typical stage robbery portrayed in western films showed the bandits galloping at full-speed across flat terrain while exchanging gunfire. In reality, the highwaymen would simply wait on a steep grade where the team of animals was going uphill at

A six-horse hitch pulling a mud wagon. The wagons could also accommodate passengers on top. *Used by permission, Utah State Historical Society.*

a walking pace. And in the western part of the country, only one-quarter of the stage wagons were Concord coaches; the majority were the less attractive "mud wagons" used on the rougher terrain of the journey.[16] And despite the exhilarating scenes on the Hollywood screen, the stage vehicles averaged about five mph—so read on.

HISTORY OF THE OVERLAND MAIL — THE DILEMMA OF GETTING MAIL TO AND FROM CALIFORNIA

After the US acquisition of the California territory following the Mexican-American War in 1848, along with the discovery of gold at Sutter's Mill, the population in California grew to 92,597 in 1850[17] (not counting the Native Americans) and 379,994 in 1860.[18] Thousands of miners and settlers who moved to California were cut off from the rest of the nation—in terms of communication, mail, and goods. This sudden population growth in California, along with a newly acquired prominence in the world, spurred a demand for a better form of communication with the folks back home. Simultaneously there was also a population increase in Oregon and Utah as settlers flocked there for new farming opportunities.

So the need for an east-west mail service became a priority. In the earlier years, the east-west mail service was provided by ocean transportation. It took an average of two hundred days for sailing ships to make the 17,000 mile trip around Cape Horn of South America.[19]

With the population rapidly growing in the West, the government established a shorter shipping mail route through the Isthmus of Panama, which included a fifty-mile trek through the jungle. Until the Panama Railroad was built in 1855, the overland route used canoes or mules to cross the isthmus, making the route fraught with disease and threats of attack by bandits. But the Isthmus of Panama route became a faster and more viable route since the trip to California could be done in forty to ninety days, depending on when the shipping and transit connections could be made for the next leg. Even with more mail routes opening up in the coming years, the Panama route carried the majority of government mail from 1849 to 1861, while the Cape Horn route remained the preferred and cheaper route for cargo.

Top: Mud wagons were used extensively on the rougher parts of the overland journey to California. These wagons were the 4WD version of the coaches. *Used by permission, Utah State Historical Society.*

Bottom: Keeping the western spirit alive, modern teamsters pull out their cherished stagecoaches for special events. Pictured here is a six-mule hitch pulling a stagecoach through Bodie at the *Friends of Bodie* event.

Many stagecoach drivers were revered but their life was hard and at times miserable, driving the same fifty- to seventy-five-mile stretch back and forth.

As the ocean mail service became more reliable with fewer problems and the transit time shortened to approximately five to six weeks from New York to San Francisco, still one problem remained—the mail only arrived on a semi-monthly schedule. And with the explosive population growth in California, the amount of annual mail also grew from approximately 6,000 letters in 1849 to over two million letters in 1859.[20]

With the semi-monthly delivery of mail, the arrival of the mail steamer into San Francisco Bay was big news and a cause for celebration for the new settlers in northern California. To alert people about the incoming mail, a signal was transmitted from Telegraph Hill using a crude marine telegraph—a semaphore. The semaphore consisted of a pole with two movable arms that made various configurations to let the locals know if a steamer or sailing ship was arriving. Local newspapers and journalists were vigorous in their efforts to be the first to greet the ship to receive the month-old news. For the return trip, they summarized the "most wanted" local news events to send back to their eastern counterparts.

Because of the necessity to communicate with the "States" in a timely manner, the development of an overland mail service between California and the rest of the nation was envisioned by many businessmen and entrepreneurs. In response, Congress authorized four different mail routes linking the settlers in California to the eastern United States in the 1850s. The decision to fund these overland mail routes was not made for financial gain for the Post Office, but it was an effort to bind the country. Without subsidies from the government, these overland stagecoach routes could not have survived on just passenger fares.

These overland mail carriers were pioneers in every sense of the word—finding the best route for travel, encountering many obstacles including prohibitive winter storms, braving Indian and bandit attacks, and building stations along the way. With mail contracts in place, numerous stage lines traversed the West in the mid-1800s as entrepreneurs competed for mail contracts and passengers.

The trails through the frontier to California were desolate and filled with many dangers.

By the end of 1858, there were two ocean routes and four major overland routes used for mail service. The four overland lines in operation were:

- George Chorpenning originally partnered with Absalom Woodward and later with John Hockaday, and provided a central route service via Salt Lake City known as the Central Overland Route. It was used by the Pony Express starting in 1860.
- John Butterfield provided a semi-weekly mail/passenger service to San Francisco through a southern route via El Paso, Texas. It was known as the Oxbow route since it was at least six hundred miles longer than the other routes to avoid the Sierra Nevada.
- Jacob Hall provided a monthly service from Kansas City, Missouri to Stockton, California via Santa Fe, New Mexico.
- James Birch provided a semi-monthly service from San Antonio, Texas to San Diego, California.

Starting in 1851, the Central Overland Route was established. The US government advertised for bids to carry monthly mail from Sacramento across the Sierra Nevada, crossing the Great Basin into Salt Lake City, Utah. The firm of Chorpenning and Woodward won the contract for a mere $14,000 to provide mail service to Salt Lake City once a month in each direction, connecting with Samuel Woodson's established mail service to Missouri.

On May 1st of 1851, this overland mail service—affectionately known as the "Jackass Mail"—utilized mules to get the mail over the Sierra Nevada. It took George Chorpenning sixteen days to cross the Sierra Nevada because of the deep snow left from the winter months. The firm chose an old emigrant route from Sacramento through Strawberry (Highway 50), over Luther Pass into Hope Valley, through Carson Valley, Nevada, then across the Forty Mile Desert to the Humboldt River to Salt Lake City.[21] They finally reached Salt Lake City on June 5th.[22]

His misfortunes continued when Absalom Woodward was killed in an Indian attack later that year. The second winter Chorpenning routed the mail through the Feather River Canyon, but his animals froze to death en route, leaving him to carry the mail on his back the last two hundred miles.[23] After these first two perilous winters, Chorpenning rerouted the mail down through Southern California in the winter months.

Map of Overland Mail Routes. *National Map Courtesy of U.S. Geological Survey, Department of the Interior.*

In 1854, Chorpenning renewed his contract for four more years but eliminated the northern Nevada route. He carried the mail on horseback, by pack mules, or wagons from San Diego over the Mormon Trail to Salt Lake City. He encountered fewer problems and made better time with the scheduled deliveries.[24]

In 1858, Chorpenning signed another four-year contract to carry the mail every two weeks from Placerville, California, crossing the Sierra Nevada, into Salt Lake City. The route was later improved to a weekly service. In the winter, Chorpenning hired John "Snowshoe" Thompson to help get the mail over the Sierra. Snowshoe Thompson was born in Norway and became a legend for carrying mail on his back through heavy snowstorms

37

on cross-country skis (called "snowshoes" back then). This route would later be used by Russell, Majors, and Waddell, of *C.O.C. & P.P.*, which later operated the Pony Express on this route in 1860.

But in 1856, it was a presidential election year, and California had become a wealthy state. Political factions were anxious to support the "golden state" and proposed the establishment of a semi-weekly mail and passenger service to California. The development of the overland stage routes was a huge undertaking requiring large sums of money to get the stage lines in place—setting up and staffing hundreds of stage stations, purchasing hundreds of stage-coaches and mud wagons, repairing roads and bridges, hiring hundreds of employees, and purchasing horses, mules, and feed. In comparison to modern terms, the stage lines could be compared to the development of fiber optic lines, which required huge start-up costs but inevitably quickened the internet speeds as compared to the archaic dial-up internet speeds—which were incredibly slow. When a minute seemed like an hour!

In 1857, John Butterfield's *Overland Mail Company* was awarded a lucrative $600,000 government contract to provide a mail and passenger service to and from California on a semi-weekly schedule with a stipulated twenty-five-day duration for each trip. This new mail contract was the largest ever awarded, and some said the choice of Butterfield's southern route was aligned with Southern sympathies because of the Civil War brewing in the background. There was much more at stake than just the mail—southern Congressmen wanted the overland route in the South, and northern Congressmen wanted it in the North. Ultimately, the route would determine the final route of the future transcontinental railroad. As a result, Butterfield's *Overland Mail Company* improved the mail frequency and delivery speeds of four to six months—around Cape Horn—to twenty-five days.

Butterfield's overland mail route would become the most famous overland mail route—later recognized as the longest stage line in the world, nearly 2,800 miles in length. After purchasing approximately one thousand horses, five hundred mules, more than one hundred Concord coaches and Celerity wagons, and hiring eight hundred men to run the operation, the first service began in 1858,

only running until 1861 when the Civil War began.[25] Butterfield was known to rely on the Celerity wagons—similar to the mud wagon—for the rougher portions of the route.

The greatest achievement for the Butterfield stage line was the duration of the trip: It averaged twenty-one to twenty-five days for the transcontinental trip. To achieve this speed, stage drivers were changed out frequently. Waterman Lilly Ormsby, a reporter for *The New York Herald*, was sent to ride and report about the inaugural trip to San Francisco. Ormsby noted that the initial service to California included distances of 30–113 miles between relays until stage stations could be built out in this hostile and uninhabited land known as the frontier.[26] These long stretches through desolate, uninhabited land required catching and herding green mules for what Ormsby called a *Cavellado*. But it should have been called a *Caballada*—referring to a remuda (a large herd of horses or mules) brought along to change out the driving-team at intervals. Where water was not available, it was hauled in by water carts on the long stretches of desert.

The Butterfield Route was six hundred to eight hundred miles longer than other routes because it avoided the Sierra Nevada—earning it the nickname of Oxbow Route. Even though this mail route did not cross the Sierra, it is worth mentioning because of its notable accomplishments.

When Texas seceded from the Union in 1861, Butterfield's *Overland Mail Company* was destroyed in one swipe, since the mail could not be carried through Texas. The company was ordered to transfer to the Central Overland Route, Union-held territory. Thus, the *C.O.C. & P.P. Express Co.* and the *Overland Mail Company* joined forces to carry the mail over the Central Overland Route for the next year. At that point, Ben Holladay purchased the holdings and took over the route to become the *Overland Stage Company*.

In today's world, when people think of stagecoaches, they naturally recall the distinguished Wells Fargo stagecoaches. *Wells, Fargo & Co.* did not operate an overland stage line until 1867, after purchasing the stage line from Ben Holladay. This stage operation was a short-lived venture with the completion of the transcontinental railroad on May 10, 1869. However, Wells Fargo did

Precious pouches of mail, filled with news and important government documents, kept California connected to the eastern states in the 1850s.

Highway robberies were a common occurrence on the stage routes. Many of the stage lines employed an armed messenger who rode "shotgun" beside the driver to help guard the coach and its contents.

operate many other "express" stage lines—providing shorter runs between cities.

These overland stage routes were huge financial endeavors for the early stage operators. Over time, these routes had utmost importance in that they were equivalent to our modern interstate highway system. These routes were used by emigrants, stagecoaches, commercial freight teams, and the US Army and Frontier Cavalry. As a result of these routes, the groundwork was laid for the transcontinental railroad. The railroad was completed in 1869 and connected California to the eastern United States following the Central Overland Route.

STAGECOACH TRAVEL

Many stagecoaches were built for transporting mail, with the comfort of passengers an afterthought. From today's perspective, crossing the frontier in a stagecoach could be perceived as an alluring form of travel. But in reality, travel in a stagecoach was only for the hardy and adventurous. On the Butterfield route, passengers could choose to go twenty-five days without an overnight stop if they were going for speed on the transcontinental journey. This required sleeping overnight in the coaches: a twenty-four/seven journey for twenty-five days.

During the 1850s, the Overland Mail routes were being established as a means of communication with California, bringing mail to California from Missouri or Texas. The length of the trip through the frontier was twenty-five to fifty days with passengers having to overnight in the coach.

In modern times, our population complains about being crammed on an airplane in their cushy, padded seats, with reclining headrests. If only they could compare it to the arduous travel in a stagecoach. With only two stops for meals each day, stagecoach passengers had to learn to sleep sitting up for days at a time.

Edmund Verney, a prominent and well-traveled British citizen, shared his memories of his first night in a Concord coach:

I can remember no night of horror equal to my first night's travel on the Overland Route. We all know how veal-and-ham pie

increases the intensity of a nightmare; and in the same way did the solid meal, bolted against time in the Strawberry Valley, affect this night's delights. An American friend, who had himself crossed the plains, had recommended me to bring an air-pillow. This became my main-stay: I sat on it by day, or interposed it between the hard side of the coach and my ragged skin and jaded bones, and by night I put my head through the hole in the middle and wore it as a collar, like a degraded Chinaman. This saved the sides of my head during my endeavours to sleep, but occasionally a heavier jolt than usual would strike the cranium violently against the roof, driving it down between my shoulders.[27]

And when the coach was at capacity with nine passengers inside the coach, Edmund Verney eloquently shared:

The coach was quite full, nine inside and one out, the greatest number ever carried on this trip. Three Mexican women and an American lady were among the passengers; the other five were miners, and proprietors of mule or wagon trains. After journeying for two or three miles, we found there was plenty to try the temper of the passengers. We began to feel cramped, the heat of the sun made us hot and irritable: and not only was there a difficulty about stowing away one's feet, but we even had to fit in our knees one with another, and then occasionally give and take pretty smart blows caused by the jostling of the carriage. Most of the men chewed tobacco, and those who occupied centre seats had to exert considerable skill to spit clear of the other passengers. Americans are generally adept in this art, but we had one or two unskillful professors, although it must be admitted that they had hardly a fair opportunity of showing off their proficiency, from the jolting of the coach. Occasionally they would unconcernedly expectorate among the baggage on the floor. The smell caused by this abominable practice was intolerable and sickening at first, until one became somewhat accustomed to it.[28]

The glamorous Hollywood depiction is starting to wear a little thin so now we jump to another trip, one taken by Samuel Clemens. Before Samuel Clemens became Mark Twain, he took a trip to Carson City on a stagecoach from Missouri with his brother, Orion.

The rough and merciless trip left such an indelible impression on Clemens that it inspired him to write about his journey in his classic book, *Roughing It*. Twain did not hesitate to share his dreadful experience through the Forty Mile Desert. The wheels of their coach sunk in the "bottomless" sand, which forced the party to rough it and walk for many miles through the desert.

Maybe not portrayed as a dangerous profession on the big screen, stagecoach drivers were revered and likened to the Roman chariot drivers from centuries ago. The job required exceptional horsemanship, driving skills, and nerves of steel while traveling through hostile Indian country. Many routes had the drivers work the same fifty- to seventy-five -mile section going back and forth,

east and west. But in reality, the life of a stagecoach driver was hard, and at times miserable. The grandeur wore off after long hours on the trail. In *Roughing It*, Mark Twain shared a story about a driver who was doing a double-shift—driving seventy-five miles in one direction and then returning back the same seventy-five miles:

I found [the] driver sound asleep on the box…the conductor said never mind him, there was no danger, and he was doing double duty…a hundred and fifty miles of holding back of six vindictive mules and keeping them from climbing the trees! It sounds incredible, but I remember the statement…[29]

The First Trip to California in the Butterfield Overland Stage

In 1858, Waterman L. Ormsby, a reporter for *The New York Herald*, was sent to ride and report about the first Butterfield Overland stage to make the inaugural 2,800-mile trip to San Francisco. Coming from New York, Ormsby had no knowledge of the West; those on the East Coast could not comprehend the snow-covered mountains in the West nor the deserts with temperatures over 100°F. As the sole passenger on that inaugural coach, the twenty-four-day trip would be raw, dangerous, and unforgiving.

Ormsby's trip through the Southwest was quite memorable and recorded from different perspectives. When they reached the Southwest, they came to a stage station that had been attacked by Indians, who had run off all the horses that were needed to replenish the spent horses. The stage would have to go on if it were to make the scheduled "contract" time and needed fresh horses. So the Butterfield men sent some Mexican herders to rope some green mules. It took two hours to rope and harness the unbroken mules. Ormsby was getting incredibly nervous thinking that the coach would be wrecked at some point, leaving him seriously injured or dead in the middle of nowhere. He offered to wait for the next stage, but the driver knew that it was imperative for Ormsby to be on that "first" stage to San Francisco. With so much fear of the oncoming situation, the conversation went something like this:

"These mules are green and want to run," Ormsby noted.

Mules and horses were used to pull the Overland Mail stagecoaches and mud wagons. The Butterfield Overland Mail Company was known for using "green" mules and mustangs.

The driver calmly replied, "We'll let them run. Maybe we'll make up some time."

"But the mules will crash us," Ormsby said.

"Hopefully they won't. They'll probably calm down after a while," the driver said.

So Ormsby decided to ride up next to the driver so he could jump if the coach tipped over. The Mexicans firmly held the heads of the mules, looked at each other grinning—thinking to themselves "this is going to be fun." The mules were frightened and frantic wanting to rid themselves of the harness and the big "beast" behind them. So all they could do was RUN when released. They tried to run in different directions, but the driver remained calm with a firm grip on the reins, keeping the mules mostly on the road. Ormsby was terrified and hanging onto the seat rail,

Life on the Overland Trail was a lonely life, traveling through the desolate frontier.

thinking he had just met his maker. It took a few miles for Ormsby to calm himself while the sun was starting to set and the road was becoming dimmer.

Ormsby then inquired, "How far till the next station?"

"It's about thirty miles," the driver replied.

"How well do you know the road?" Ormsby asked.

"I don't know the road, I've never been over it before," the driver said.

"Then how do you expect to get there?" the reporter demanded.

"There's only one road, and if there's only one, how can you miss it?" he replied.[30]

Out in the desolate frontier, these two men were in very unfamiliar territory wandering over a pair of wagon tracks, not so much a road, as the moon slowly came up.

After reaching San Francisco, Ormsby was not shy about sharing his opinion: "Had I not just come out over the route, I would be perfectly willing to go back, but I know what Hell is like. I've just had 24 days of it."[31] After his ordeal on the frontier, Ormsby returned to New York by steamer.

Stage Wagons and Coaches

The stagecoaches used on the flatter portions of the overland routes were built by the Abbot-Downing Company in Concord, New Hampshire, and were commonly referred to as Concord coaches. The Concord coaches had a reputation of being superior to other coaches, known for their durability, overall quality, and handsome appearance. The coaches were equipped with three bench seats accommodating nine passengers inside, one or two on the box next to the driver, and an additional person on top. These masterpiece coaches cost $1,200–1,500, weighed 2,500 pounds, and were individually numbered. The Concord coaches were the first to offer "thoroughbrace" suspension—each coach rested on two ox-hide leather straps, called thoroughbraces, that acted as shock absorbers and were less jarring than coaches made with steel spring suspension. Rocking like ships in a storm, some passengers were sick part of the journey, adding another dimension to their grueling saga across the frontier.

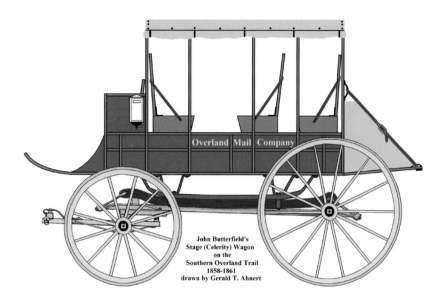

John Butterfield's
Stage (Celerity) Wagon
on the
Southern Overland Trail
1858-1861
drawn by Gerald T. Ahnert

The celerity wagon was a lighter stage vehicle with the wheels set further apart, to prevent it from tipping over. John Butterfield had 100 Celerity wagons built for his overland route since the wagons were designed for faster speed. *Image credit: Wikimedia, Gerald Ahnert.*

The celebrated stagecoach was known for its elegant curves and beauty but in reality "mud wagons" were the preferred stage vehicle for the rough terrain in the West. As indicated by the name, mud wagons were not as elegant but were designed to travel over rougher trails and roads during inclement weather. There are some variations among the mud wagons, but in general they were lighter in weight, weighing eight hundred to 1,200 pounds; boxier in design; had a lower center of gravity and a wider wheelbase; were built with an outside frame; and were less expensive to build. These semi-enclosed wagons were equipped with leather or canvas side curtains rather than glass windows, which offered little protection from dust and rain.

The Celerity stage wagon was another variation of a mud wagon used extensively on the Butterfield Overland Trail. It had a lighter frame structure with a canvas covering allowing for better airflow, but the overall design was built for speed.

Stagecoaches and mud wagons were pulled with four or six horses or mules with an average speed of 5 mph for overland travel, with each driver covering sixty to seventy miles on average. The horses were changed for fresh stock at each station, which were usually about ten to twenty miles apart.

Horse Hitches

The typical overland stage was pulled by six horses or mules, made up of three pairs of animals. The pair of horses closest to the coach was called wheel horses or "wheelers" and were usually the largest of the pairs. The wheelers provided the braking power—slowing the vehicle while going downhill. The wheelers also steered the vehicle by turning the shafts or pole. The next pair in the center was called the "swing" horses. The front horses were called the "leaders" and usually the smallest horses. It took extraordinary skill to handle a six-horse hitch, since each horse was controlled by an individual rein—with three individual reins in each hand. When driving a mountain trail, the driver, using only his reins, had to turn each pair of animals separately, so the pairs did not become tangled resulting in an overturned stagecoach.

Despite the exhilarating scenes on the Hollywood screen, the stage vehicles averaged about five mph. *Drawing courtesy of Mary Kimmel.*

After cresting the Sierra at Luther Pass, the Pony Express re-enactment rider enters the Eastern Sierra and the Nevada portion of the Sierra Nevada, following the old Pony Express trail.

CHAPTER FOUR

THE PONY EXPRESS: AMERICAN HEROES OF THE FRONTIER

Just like the story of Paul Revere's ride—an actual historical event that has been retold and adorned over the years—the legendary story of the Pony Express has evolved into layers of truth embedded with myths. But it's one of the quintessential stories that represent the spirit of the Old American West, at a time when it was expanding and evolving. There was not one hero to identify with, but the riders as a whole became a symbol of American pride.

But how did the story of the Pony Express come about? The idea and installation of the Pony Express did not come about overnight; it took some daring risks and ill-conceived ideas that ultimately resulted in the final operation. In 1855, William Russell, Alexander Majors, and William Waddell formed a partnership that was awarded a government contract to deliver supplies to the military posts on the western frontier. This first contract enabled their firm to become the largest freighting company west of Missouri.

In 1857, they received their second contract with the government, but the outbreak of the Utah War or "Mormon War" caused some financial difficulties for the company.

Then the news of the Pike's Peak Gold Rush in 1858 had Russell convinced that he should find a way to capitalize on it. He partnered up with John S. Jones and launched an express-passenger service in the Rocky Mountains—running between Leavenworth and Denver (a 680-mile route). The new service was named Leavenworth City & Pike's Peak Express Company: *L. & P. P. Express Co.* for short. Money was borrowed for this new venture so they could buy fifty new Concord coaches and eight hundred mules to pull the coaches.[32] Unfortunately, the emigrants that came to the area arrived by wagon train or on foot. In 1859, *L. & P. P. Express Co.* purchased Hockaday & Company's semi-monthly contract to transport mail between Missouri and Salt Lake City. Following this purchase, they abandoned the Leavenworth-Denver Route. Russell was an ambitious businessman, and this purchase put him closer to one of his goals—a contract to carry the US mail to California over the Central Overland Route.[33] The expenses involved with adding stations to this route caused some financial hardships for Russell, which threatened the credit reputation of the Russell, Majors, and Waddell firm.

Russell did not consult with Majors and Waddell before he entered into the *L. & P. P. Express Co.* venture and accumulated some serious debt. So in late 1859, Russell, Majors, and Waddell reorganized their partnership—assuming the debts and assets of *L. & P. P. Express Co.*—and named Russell as the president of the firm. On a trip back East to raise capital for this new firm, Russell decided to name the new firm Central Overland California & Pike's Peak Express Company or *C.O.C. & P.P. Express Co.* To make matters worse, Russell informed his son (not his partners) the following: "Having determined to establish a Pony Express to Sacramento, California, commencing 3rd of April. Time ten days."

It has been debated who was the brainchild of the Pony Express. Many accepted that Benjamin Ficklin came up with the idea, who passed it on to Senator William Gwin, who passed it on to Russell. We may never know who conceived the original idea of the Pony Express but historians agree as to who put the plan into action: William Russell.

Map of Pony Express Route. *National Map Courtesy of U.S. Geological Survey, Department of the Interior.*

On January 27, 1860, Russell, Majors, and Waddell announced the formation of *C.O.C. & P.P. Express Co.* and their plans for a fast, direct mail service between St. Joseph, Missouri and Sacramento, California.[34] This madcap idea—a proposal of covering 1,966 miles in ten days—would be accomplished with a twenty-four-hour relay of fast, lightweight riders using the existing stage route.[35] Many said that this lightning-fast mail service—later becoming known as the Pony Express—would be an impossible feat.

With only sixty days to prepare for the ride, wagon trains were sent to construct the relay stations needed along the route. Additional horses had to be purchased, while simultaneously recruiting eighty riders for the overland journey. The *C.O.C. & P.P. Express Co.* was looking to recruit expert riders willing to risk death. They might

achieve fame but not fortune since the pay varied from $50 to $150 per month.[36] Eye-catching notices were posted in newspapers: "Wanted. Young, Skinny, Wiry Fellows not over 18."

It was a huge undertaking, but once the route was equipped, it was comprised of approximately one hundred fifty stations, four hundred to five hundred horses, and eighty riders.[37] The mail service started as a weekly mail service and later changed to a semi-weekly schedule.

For an average ride of the relay, the ride utilized three remount stations and three additional horses while covering up to seventy-five miles, with only two minutes allowed for changing horses and mail at each station.[38] To achieve this quick change of horses, a specially designed leather mochila (Spanish for knapsack) was used to transport the mail. It could hold letters and newspapers weighing up to twenty pounds. As an extra precaution against the weather, the mail was wrapped in oiled silk. The mochila was placed over the saddle and could be removed and transferred to another horse in a quick exchange. The desired weight of the rider, mail, and mochila was 165 pounds.

But the stories about the mail exchange varied widely. In 1861 "Bronco Charlie" Miller—who claimed to be only eleven years old when he rode between Sacramento and Placerville—stated that each rider rode thirty-five to seventy-five a day, which also included night riding.[39] Other sources state the average mileage for each rider was seventy-five miles. Comparing different historical journals and quotes, there were different average speeds recorded—ranging from 8 mph to 10 mph—for the ten-day journey.

After much publicity and fanfare, on April 3, 1860 the first Pony Express relay ride left both St. Joseph and Sacramento to cheering crowds. The rider going westbound was delayed since the St. Joseph train arrived late that day with the mail. Two hours later, the rider departed St. Joseph as a cannon was fired to commemorate the big ceremony; the mail arrived in Sacramento ten days later.

In the eastward direction, the mail left San Francisco on a steamer on the Sacramento River, meeting up with the first rider in Sacramento. With enthusiastic crowds in the background, the mail pouch was given to Harry Roff and he began the perilous journey out of Sacramento. The trail out of Sacramento was a steady climb for almost one hundred miles, climbing over 7,000 feet in elevation to cross the mighty Sierra Nevada.[40] Harry Roff and Sam Hamilton made that climb through the Sierra through thirty feet of snow—the

"Galloping off into the horizon, as quick as they came,
The pony rider's integrity is laced with lots of luck and trust.
With the precious mail tucked neatly inside 'La Mochila,'
They left behind only tracks, a weary horse and some dust."

—Sallie Knowles Joseph

mule trains kept the trails packed down in the winter making travel by horseback possible.[41] The mail arrived in St. Joseph ten days later to much commotion and celebration—with folks eagerly calculating the rate per mile of the journey.

After the first successful Pony rides, the mail service became invaluable with the Civil War approaching. The folks in California eagerly awaited to receive the news of Lincoln's election and inauguration. By November of 1860, the telegraph line had been built to Fort Kearny, Nebraska on the east end and near Carson City, Nevada on the west end. Special arrangements had been made to expedite the mail for the election results. In special honor of the ride, the riders and horses were decorated with ribbons. News announcing the election of President Lincoln traveled the route in an amazing seven days—the greatest achievement of the Pony Express.

The astonishing seven-day feat generated a lot of publicity, but in the end, the mail service never turned a profit. The service was costly for everyday folks; it cost $5 for a half-ounce of mail (equivalent to $130 today) and was later reduced to $1. So the service was mostly used to deliver newspapers, business documents, and government dispatches printed on tissue paper to keep the costs minimized. In addition to the overwhelming operational and startup costs, there were many challenges with managing the mail service.

In 1860, the first winter was a hard winter for the Pony Express, testing its financial stability as it struggled with heavy debt. The *C.O.C. & P.P. Express Co.* informed the public that service during the winter would be longer in duration—it took an additional fifteen days travel time to San Francisco.[42] Heavy snows hit the Sierra Nevada in December, but some of the mining traffic kept the trails beaten down, leaving the Sierra Nevada somewhat passable. But the less-traveled mountains of the Great Basin did not have traffic packing down the trails in the snowstorms, so these areas were impassable while causing long delays. As the winter wore on, there was more heavy snowpack delaying the ride up to another four days.[43]

Trying to overcome the financial instability, bond scandals, and heavy debt, the demise of the Pony Express was inevitable, but the final dagger came with the completion of the transcontinental telegraph line. In late October of 1861, the telegraph connecting the East and West met up in Salt Lake City. Despite its reputation as an Old West legend, this nearly impossible human and horse feat only lasted eighteen months while never turning a profit.

Even with its short life on the frontier, the Pony Express made 308 rides each way, carried 35,000 pieces of mail, and covered 616,000 miles.[44] When the Pony Express came to an end, *C.O.C. & P.P. Express Co.* had $400,000 of debt. After its abrupt ending, Ben Holladay purchased the company and stage line once the company went into foreclosure.

Undeterred after its demise, the public did not forget the heroic saga of the Pony Express. The legend of the Pony Express carried on for years, with the characters taking on a larger than life role, conjuring up images of riders at break-neck speeds carrying important mail while simultaneously shooting their Winchester rifles in the air. The stories became more embellished as they were passed down among the generations of followers, adding to the American folklore.

This everlasting image of the Pony Express was cultivated by William "Buffalo Bill" Cody and his Wild West vaudeville shows in the 1880s. Even though Buffalo Bill claimed to have been a Pony Express rider—alleging that he once rode 384 miles in a single run—historians have not been able to document his participation. Regardless of Cody's involvement with the Pony Express, he kept the memory alive.

"Relentless in desire, the loyal horse and rider sped…
'The mail must go through' even if life be the cost,
With bravery and courage and the will of a saint,
The trail of the Mochila was never tarnished or lost."

—Sallie Knowles Joseph

Left: This rider is starting her leg of the Pony Express—the mochila is presented well in this photo. You can see two of the four cantinas, where the mail is stored.

When the Pony Express first started its service, many thought it was just a publicity stunt. But in the end, the Pony Express mail service accomplished record-setting speeds for overland travel at a time when many regarded it as an impossible feat.

Go Pony!

THE ANNUAL PONY EXPRESS RE-RIDE

The National Pony Express Association hosts an annual Commemorative Re-Ride of the Pony Express Trail from Sacramento, California to St. Joseph, Missouri. The Re-Ride takes place in June coinciding with the full moon, so the night riders have some moonlight to help light their way. The ride alternates in direction each year: riding west-to-east one year followed by east-to-west the following year.

The Re-Ride is a ten-day, twenty-four-hours per day, non-stop relay that covers the 1,966-mile route of the Pony Express National Historic Trail traveling through eight states—California, Nevada, Utah, Wyoming, Nebraska, Colorado, Kansas, and Missouri. The route is designated as a historic trail and administered by the National Park Service.

Each year approximately seven hundred riders participate in the Re-Ride, helping to carry the commemorative letters along the historic trail. Commemorative letters can be purchased through the National Pony Express Association (NPEA). Each envelope is hand-stamped with a special US Post Office cancellation and is an official souvenir from each year's ride. Also, the letters are designated for each state, providing a means of fundraising. The letters are carried in the official mochila—a removable leather cover with four pouches to even out the load and placed over the horse's saddle; the mochila is passed on from each rider. Modern Pony Express riders still don the official Pony Express uniform—a red shirt, chocolate brown vest, yellow scarf, jeans, boots, and a western hat or helmet. Additionally, new riders are inducted into the National Pony Express Association by taking the oath of the Pony Express.

The Pony Express Oath

I do hereby swear, before the great and living God, that during my employment as a Pony Express rider, I will under no circumstances use profane language, drink intoxicating liquors, abuse my mount, quarrel

The Pony Express is a ten-day, twenty-four-hour relay that runs through the nighttime. Horses have very good night vision but the riders have to learn to adapt to the night riding. The Re-Ride coincides with a full moon in the month of June.

or fight with any other riders and so that in every respect, I will conduct myself honestly, be faithful to my duties, and so direct my acts to win the confidence of everyone.

Every year ham radio plays a vital role in the Re-Ride by providing communications along the trail, which is very important in the remote parts of the trail where cell phone coverage is non-existent. This communication helps the ride captains keep tabs on the ride and if the mail is on time. Additionally, a GPS unit is carried in the mochila along with the mail, pinging the mochila location every twenty minutes. These modern communications provide information to the online Pony Express Tracking Map, which helps spectators follow the progress of the mail on the trail.

In addition to the ride re-enactment, the NPEA also plays an important role in the trail maintenance, marking the trail, and providing educational events to help celebrate this remarkable historic feat. More information about the Re-Ride can be found online at: https://nationalponyexpress.org.

Compared to the original Pony Express ride, in which riders rode a seventy-five-mile segment two times per week while willing to risk death on each leg, the annual Re-Ride is a fairly controlled environment. Present-day riders select the length they would prefer to ride—from one to twenty miles for each leg—and the riders are encouraged to ride their leg ahead of time to become familiar with the trail. Additionally, the ride is divided into sections, with a ride captain assigned to oversee the riders in their section. There is a support vehicle that travels along with the riders for most of the route. The Re-Ride tries to achieve the original average speed of the historic riders, 10 mph, but sometimes there are unexpected obstacles or unforeseen challenges along the route that can impede the average speed of the Re-Ride.

In 2017 in the Sierra Nevada, the winter storms had produced record snowfalls, leaving the Sierra still snow-covered at the higher elevations in June. The riders had to navigate a trail through the deep snow-pack ahead of time—in some places, the snowpack was three feet deep. Near Lake Tahoe at Johnson Grade, Jerry Bestpitch was scouting for his second leg of the trail in the deep snowpack; the ride was going the east-to-west direction that year and Jerry was riding two legs in the area. He was called and notified that the Nevada riders were three hours ahead of schedule and that he needed to be in place for his first leg, at the Nevada border, ahead of his designated time for the Re-Ride. He hastily got into position…. and then waited…and waited for another hour and a half.

Wondering what the hold-up was, he learned that the rider had an unexpected dismount coming down from Kingsbury Grade and the horse took off into the mountains, along with the mochila and mail. This was in an undeveloped part of the Sierra Nevada east of the Lake Tahoe area—with miles of hills for a horse to run and explore. Jerry called some nearby riders and a support team to help him look for the horse. Losing the mailbag would be a tragic event, so they looked with absolute determination. After an hour and a half of searching, the fire department called to let the riders know that the horse had made it to one of the outlying neighborhoods in the Lake Tahoe basin and was wandering around in the backyards.

I'm sure the homeowners are still re-telling the story of how the Pony Express re-routed the trail through their backyard that year. But with a three-hour lead time, the Pony Express was back on track to make it to Sacramento in the allotted time.

Another story worth sharing occurred in northern Nevada, east of the Sierra Nevada, where there is a large population of wild horses, which the riders sometimes have to contend with en route. Additionally, the riders have one of the toughest sections of the Pony Express in a very remote area that tops 8,000 feet in elevation. My friend, Tony Zamora, shared with me a story about his encounter with wild horses. He was riding his mare, Desi, when they approached a band of wild horses. Each band of wild horses is made up of a stallion and his harem of mares and his younger offspring. The stallion noticed Tony and the mare off in the distance—over a quarter-mile away. The stallion had a strong interest in Tony's mare and started to communicate with Desi. Tony noted, "I don't know what he said to her but he put her in a trance and she came to a halt mesmerized by this stallion. So there I was on the ground—pulling her along, cussin' up a storm, and airin' out my lungs. A bit of a challenge when you're trying to make 8 to 10 mph on the trail."

Rattlesnakes, heat, bear encounters, and riding at night also present challenges along the trail. Since the ride goes twenty-four/seven, riders have to learn to ride in the dark. The horses are quite adept at riding at night, as they have better night vision than humans. I've heard about riders taking along a flashlight, lantern, or glow stick to help them navigate the darkness. Sallie Joseph shared with me her story about wearing a headlamp: "I had on one of those LED headlamps, but it made a strong, bright line on the ground in front of my horse. It spooked my horse, so I had to ride the whole ten miles with my head held high—keeping my chin way up, which is not the most ideal riding position."

If you want to be a part of this legendary ride, you will need to become a member of the NPEA by contacting one of the division's located in either California, Nevada, Utah, Wyoming, Nebraska, Colorado, Kansas, or Missouri. You can ride a leg of the route or be a part of the support crew. For more information, please visit the National Pony Express website at https://nationalponyexpress.org/annual-re-ride/.

Top: Capturing a moment in time along the Pony Express Re-Ride.

Top left: A Pony Express rider slows down to take in the view of Lake Tahoe on Johnson Pass.

Bottom left: Gorgeous views of the Sierra Nevada along the California section of the Pony Express route.

51

A woman hands off a letter to a Pony Express rider (in a re-enactment event).

The Pony Express Story – by Sallie Knowles Joseph

The poster read "WANTED—young, skinny, wiry fellows,
To ride from Missouri to California in ten days or less---
Must be excellent horsemen and willing to risk death daily,
Carrying the mail cross-country for The Pony Express…"

In bold print it also emphasized "Orphans Preferred,"
The Overland Mail service requires men with heart…
A pony rider must be brimful of endurance and spirit,
Morally sound, weatherproof, brave, tough, and smart.

The legend of "The Pony" overshadows its brief life,
Russell, Majors, and Waddell's idea was worth fighting for…
History was made by spreading the news quickly,
To bind a nation that was being threatened by war.

As gold was discovered in California the population exploded,
The need for news became desperate as the West grew.
Emigrants, miners, and settlers needed a message service,
And so The Pony Express began—the mail must go through.

Majors planned out the trail starting in the East heading West,
Over the Missouri, across Nebraska territory along the Platte,
Then on to Wyoming and dipping down into Colorado,
Then traveling along through Utah and the Great Salt Lake Flat.

On and on the route continued through the Great Basin Country,
Spanning the dry deserts of Nevada and the rugged Sierra…
A one thousand nine hundred sixty-six mile connection,
Between Missouri and San Francisco—to dawn a new Era.

Home stations were established every 75 to 100 miles,
With relay points to change to fresh horses every 10 to 15—
They hired riders, packers, for supplies and handlers for mail,
Also station keepers and stock tenders to man the sites in between.

The horses were selected for their speed and endurance,
Two hundred gray mares started the Pony Express band,
In addition Thoroughbreds, Morgans, and Mustangs,
Made up the scattered remuda wearing the XP brand.

The mail was carried in a "Mochila," Spanish for knapsack—
With locked cantinas so the mail wouldn't get stolen or lost.
The leather saddle cover protected tissue paper letters,
And an expensive five dollars an ounce was the initial cost.

In the 18 months from April 3, 1860 to October 26, 1861,
The Pony Express made the uniting of the states a success.
Carrying the news of the beginning of the Civil War,
And also the poignant words of Lincoln's inaugural address.

After the secession of Texas closed all the southern routes,
The Pony Express lifeline seemed to be the obvious trend.
But the Congress gave the mail contract to the Overland,
And The Pony began to feel the beginning of the end.

THEN THE WIRES TOUCHED –

With the completion of the Transcontinental Telegraph,
The Pony Express ceased operation on October 26, 1861…
But the linking of communication to unite a nation,
Was an instrumental achievement in how the West was won!

© Sallie Knowles Joseph

Pony Express riders participate in many parades and community events throughout the year. Pictured are Pony Express riders participating in the Hangtown Christmas parade.

A Nevada Pony Express rider in the Eastern Sierra.

The qualities of a cowboy symbolize the traits and spirit of the American West: strength, courage, and self-reliance. The days of the frontier may be long gone, but the pioneer spirit lives on through the legend of the iconic cowboy.

CHAPTER FIVE

COWBOYS & CATTLE DRIVES IN THE SIERRA NEVADA

THE COWBOY

The characters of the Old West—cowboys, outlaws, miners, gunslingers, lawmen, bounty hunters—have captured our romantic imaginations for generations and filled many dime novels along with a bustling Western film genre. Over the years, the cowboy has been depicted as a free-spirited soul who freely roamed the wide-open frontier of the lawless West. There is no shortage of myths related to this national icon who has been sensationalized and become a metaphor for America's frontier. In modern times, John Wayne, Ronald Reagan, and the Marlboro ads reinvented the genre and kept the romanticism alive in our heads.

But removing the fictional virtues of the sensationalized cowboy, the actual heritage of the American cowboy is celebrated at many western and historical museums as a national icon, but in a more truthful light. In reality, the role of the cowboy should involve the mundane duties of animal husbandry in addition to his excellent horsemanship and superior work ethic. Just as the romanticized cowboy wandered through the vast frontier, today he manages cattle on open rangeland—in rugged areas that still capture our idealist views of the West. In short, we are still captivated by the steadfast cowboy who has held on to the western traditions passed down from many generations of hardworking folks.

Before the Mexican territory was ceded to the United States, vaqueros rode the ranges and managed the large domesticated herds of cattle in what is now California, Arizona, New Mexico, and Texas. The term vaquero—meaning a Mexican cowboy or herdsmen—was

derived from the Spanish word *vaca*, meaning cow. Many of the American cowboy's skills, gear, and terminology are rooted in the vaquero techniques, including leather chaps, branding, remuda, hackamore, mustang, bronco, tapaderas, riata or lariat, dally, and their distinctive saddles. Experienced vaqueros were renowned for their exceptional roping and riding skills and taught the inexperienced Anglo settlers of the West how to round up cattle, bring down a steer with ropes, and break a wild horse.

In many parts of the Mexican territory, large numbers of semi-feral cattle roamed the open range. One of their annual traditions was to round up the young calves for branding in the spring, along with sorting the other cattle to sell. This procedure required expert horsemanship, supreme roping skills, and specially trained "cutting" horses—trained to stop and turn with the movements of a cow. These round-ups could require days of work and many fresh horse mounts, which brought about the concept of the remuda. On a big range, the

Left: Moving the cattle with the dramatic Ritter Range in the background in the Eastern Sierra.

Bottom: A glorious sunset is the reward for a full-day's work on the trail.

vaquero would need to change out horses a few times a day, to keep them rested for the next day. Therefore, they brought along a herd of horses, called a remuda, to change out their horse mounts.

Today these open-range techniques are extensively used on the ranches and the rangelands of the West. In the United States, the terms cowboy, buckaroo, cowpoke, cowhand, and cowpuncher have roughly the same meaning—but they might be used in different regions. The term buckaroo is a corruption of the word vaquero, probably derived from *bukra* from the Gullah dialect; today the term buckaroo is used extensively throughout the Great Basin.

The role of the cowboy or cowgirl today demands hardworking individuals with unparalleled work ethics. The job is hard, dangerous, dirty, and at times very rewarding—but not materialistic rewards. The job requires excellent horsemanship, being skilled with the riata or lariat, and working endless hours. The cowhands are responsible for feeding, branding, and moving cattle and horses to different pastures. In addition, they do odd jobs such as fixing fences or doing repairs around the ranch. The work of a cowboy or cowgirl is never done, since they are always on call—making their life similar to the cowboys of the past.

Even though the role of the modern cowboy is similar to cowhands from one hundred years ago, the modern cowboy has evolved with the times. Some of the larger cattle operations now use cattle management software to help effectively manage their herd. And with better cell coverage, the cowboys use their cellphones as a means to communicate with the ranch or outside world.

There are many people in different parts of the country who think the cowboy is a dying breed and are not even aware of the open rangeland that still exists in the West today. As one rancher told me, "there will always be cowboys as long as there are cattle, because the tried-and-true way to work cattle is from horseback." In the United States, cattle operations are still one of the largest segments in American agriculture, with more than one million beef producers.

RANCHING IN THE SIERRA NEVADA

California has more than 100 million acres of land, with 38 million acres available for range and pasture lands, half of which is managed by the federal government. With the different climates in California, the state has rangeland that is classified as Intermountain, Mediterranean, and desert. In the Sierra Nevada, the cattle typically graze at lower elevations in the winter and spring, and are then moved to higher elevations during summer. In the fall, cattle graze on residual rangeland or pasture forage. The different regional factors influence the type of cattle breed and nutritional requirements. Most ranches in California are family owned and have been in the same family for multiple generations.

In recent years, there was some bad press that shortsightedly labeled ranchers as being destructive to the environment. With careful grazing and sound management techniques, ranchers can be incredible stewards of the land. The livelihood of ranchers depends on healthy natural resources which in turn benefits the wildlife. Making water improvements, using rotational grazing, and planting trees have benefited the environment. There have been many studies

Six generations of the Cashbaugh family carry on the traditions passed down from a century ago.

The fall months can bring unpredictable weather in the Sierra Nevada. Cowboys have to be prepared to work in all types of conditions throughout the year—unseasonably cold weather, snow, intense heat, gusty winds, and dust storms.

that have shown that controlled livestock grazing enhances the quality of forage for deer, elk, and antelope in the western states. Other benefits from controlled grazing include: reducing wildfire threats, improving vegetation along stream banks, control of invasive plant species, and habitat restoration for threatened or endangered species. In California, there is a huge problem with invasive plant species; a coordinated effort with ranchers can help produce effective rangeland conservation.

But in California, the rancher is confronted with many extraordinary challenges that make it difficult for the rancher to succeed. With soaring land costs, fewer lease permits, more government regulations, increasing environmental pressures, and less water available, the obstacles are becoming a paramount concern for the next generation. As an example, recently the Owens Valley and Long Valley ranch lessees in the Eastern Sierra have been subjected to more water restrictions dictated by the Los Angeles Department of Water & Power. The water wars in southern California started in the early 1900s and will never improve as a growing population has a larger thirst for more water.

CATTLE GATHERS AND DRIVES

As seen on the silver screen, in old Westerns like *Red River*, we witnessed cattle drives that endured Indian attacks, thrilling gunfights, heart-pounding stampedes, and endless dust. But Hollywood tended to exaggerate the dangers associated with driving cattle—well, except for the dust.

A cattle drive is a traditional method of moving cattle a long distance, with riders directing the animals on horseback. Cattle drives can be a few miles to a few hundred miles in length. Today many cattle owners move their cattle by truck, but there are still a few cattle drives in operation that utilize this time-honored practice—moving the cattle to a summer or fall location. Originating in Mexico, the vaqueros rounded up and moved their semi-feral cattle over long distances on horseback. In the latter part of the 1800s, large cattle drives were a necessity, when thousands of head of cattle were moved from Texas to the Kansas railhead—establishing the historic Chisholm Trail. The advent of the barbed wire and the numerous rail lines eliminated the need for these nostalgic, long trail drives.

Moving and sorting the cattle into the corrals.

Flank riders keep the herd together without bunching up too much. The Drag riders keep the herd moving from the rear.

One of the rewards of a cowhand's job are the special memories: the drum of hoofbeats at sunset on the dusty trail while the colorful mountains change their hue.

Today few true cattle drives remain in California, with most being smaller in scale. The Hunewill Ranch, for example, offers a drive as part of their dude ranch, along with a few smaller drives in the Eastern Sierra, Bakersfield area, western Sierra, and coastal region. Also, there is less of a need to drive the cattle long distances on horseback with the development of the modern cattle truck and ATVs. However, there is still a need to round up and gather cattle in adjacent pastures or on leased land, which is quite prevalent in California. Stories from the older generation are slowly fading away. These stories recounted a time when the ranges were wide open, and thousands of head of cattle were moved long distances with only a few cowhands and their trusty dogs.

THE YRIBARREN CATTLE GATHER & DRIVE

The aroma of bacon and freshly brewed coffee over a sagebrush fire, mixed with the cold mountain air, is one of the delights in the High Sierra—signaling the start of a new day filled with much promise. Tucked away up in Coyote Flat, we are in an old cow camp that has hosted many cattle gathers and drives since the late 1800s. An iconic relic from a century ago is the old cow camp cabin that has sheltered many cowboys in early snowstorms and been the backdrop

for many campfire stories—a place to hear many tall tales of legendary cowboys who outmaneuvered death in the Sierra Nevada.

The fall air is getting crisper, signaling the seasonal ritual of bringing the cows down from the high country. After a hearty breakfast and some strong cowboy coffee, one of the cowhands whistles at his cow dog from his horse and they hit the trail. It is still fairly dark, as the sun and moonlight dance back and forth for a few minutes in the predawn hour. The sun eventually wins out and gently paints the mountains in soft pink and peach hues, as we each gasp at our sublime view. But this breathtaking painting is a fleeting moment, as the sun quickly changes its palette to brilliant, gold tones. It's hard to remind ourselves that it's just another magnificent sunrise in the High Sierra, with some mornings more colorful than others.

The other cowboys quickly mount their horses and help scout for cows that have spent the summer in the glorious high country. It's time to signal to the older cows that know the trail well, that it's time to go home—until next season. The experienced cowhands round up the cows hidden up in the trees and bring them to the center of the big valley. The next trick is to get one of the older cows to make the trek up the steep chute to the next valley above, and on to the 10,300-foot pass. Hopefully, the younger cows will follow with their calves in tow, making everyone's job easier.

As I watch these cowboys and cowgirls work the cattle, the spirits of the Old West make their presence known as we retrace the historic cow and sheep trails used by cowboys and old sheepherders from another era. It's hard to contain my excitement, but I have to keep ahead of the cowboys in a side-by-side while trying to get my cameras ready—hoping to capture one of those special moments. My friend, Chuck Scott, expertly maneuvers the side-by-side through many washed out trails and roads as he yells, "Hold on tight." Along the way, he shares many stories from years ago about this historic Yribarren Cattle Gather and Drive. He went to high school with Ronnie Yribarren and visited the ranch in Bishop regularly in the summers when Ronnie's dad, Louie Yribarren, owned the ranch.

The Yribarren family—proud Basque ranchers—has owned this cattle operation for almost fifty years. Ronnie Yribarren took over the operation twenty-nine years ago after the passing of his father. After working on the ranch for most of his life, Ronnie is retiring after many years of hard labor, dedication, and an assortment of physical injuries—an incredibly hard decision since it's in his blood. You can see the absolute joy he has when he's out working with the cattle or cowhands. There is never a dull moment around Ronnie; when not giving commands in regards to the cattle, he keeps everyone on their toes with his quick wit and spontaneous humor. And at times he can be in pain from his numerous injuries over the years, but he perseveres without missing a beat.

They say there are cultural heritage and traditions passed on to future generations developed on each family ranch. I wholeheartedly agree, but there is another benefit from many of these family ranches (and pack stations) that I have observed—they have life-changing effects on those who work there. I have seen many cowboys and packers become large animal veterinarians, horse trainers, range consultants, writers, poets, teamsters, rodeo superstars, and a Western Music Hall of Fame singer because of their experiences at the ranch or pack station where they learned good cowboy work ethics and bettered themselves as a person.

Additionally, I have heard many stories about how Ronnie and Cathy Yribarren have touched the lives of those who had reached

"My saddle will never be empty for it holds
the memories of the many trails gone by…
like a roadmap – it keeps the history of a journey."

—Sallie Knowles Joseph

Ronnie Yribarren and his good friend, Rob, talk about a herding strategy. Moving the cattle down from the mountains requires knowledge of animal behavior, the historic trails, and stockmanship.

Pushing the cows up the chute to the next valley.

"Cowboys need nothin' more than a hat, a horse, and the will to ride." —Anonymous

This old cow camp cabin has been used by cowboys in the high country since the early 1900s.

Early morning hues create fleeting color palettes in the Sierra.

A beautiful sunrise with the Palisades in the background.

Five generations of the Erickson family carry on the traditions passed down from the Carlon generation, in the late 1800s. *Photo Credit: Rebecca Harvey.*

the bottom depths and pulled themselves out of their despair and became better people because of them. There may not be awards hanging on the walls reflecting the influence of these ranch owners and pack-station owners, but you see it in the pride and accomplishments of their former ranch hands.

ERICKSON FAMILY CATTLE DRIVE

The sound of cattle hooves on the highway, as cows mosey on their way down from the summer meadows, with cars passing in disbelief, is an annual tradition for the Erickson family of La Grange, California. The Erickson family cattle drive has been going on since the late 1800s. Tim Erickson's grandfather, Tim Carlon, was born near Groveland, California in 1858. Carlon's father tragically drowned in Yosemite Valley, so Carlon went to work in the local mines and at various ranch jobs to help support the family.

In 1896, Carlon purchased Stone Meadow and a portion of the Ackerson Meadows, which is now owned by Yosemite National Park, for his cattle operations. Today the Erickson family still owns Stone Meadow, which is located near the entrance to Yosemite, and it's used as a cow camp and gathering meadow in the fall. Besides raising cattle, Carlon also ran three hundred head of horses up to Yosemite National Park every summer (to be used by the park) in the 1920s. In the winter and spring, he brought the horses down to the Snelling area and leased them out for farm work—helping to plow the fields.

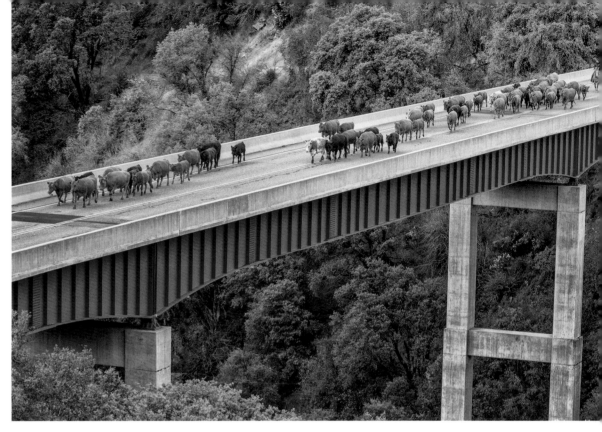

"We usually encounter between four hundred to five hundred cars and trucks that go through and around the cattle in both directions. We have a rider with a red flag out in front of the herd as well as from behind to slow the traffic and explain the situation" Erickson says. *Photo Credit: Rebecca Harvey.*

Moving the cattle across the Cliff House Bridge over the South Fork of Tuolumne River on Highway 120, on the Erickson Family Drive. *Photo Credit: Rebecca Harvey.*

Today five generations of the Erickson family carry on the traditions passed down from the Carlon generation. Tim Erickson is a third-generation cattle rancher and his son, Dan, is the fourth generation. Following in his footsteps, Dan's children are now involved with the ranch operations and cattle drives.

Tim Erickson shares, "On our fall cattle drive, we move about five hundred-plus head of cattle for six days. Most of the route is cross-country or on small county roads. But we have to travel on Highway 120 for seven miles on the second day. We usually encounter between four hundred to five hundred cars and trucks that go through and around the cattle, in both directions. We do our best to help traffic pass through safely. Sometimes it gets a little hectic on the highway but the tourists, for the most part, really enjoy it. We have a rider with a red flag out in front of the herd as well as from behind to slow the traffic and explain the situation."

I'm sure that most tourists and city folks have no idea that cattle have been driven up and down that highway for more than a century. It's a family tradition that I hope continues for another one hundred years!

HUNEWILL CATTLE DRIVE

While the Old West captures our imagination with vivid images of cowboys moving cattle into the sunset, for others it's a reality, a daily job that lasts from sunup to sundown. The Hunewill Guest Ranch, located near Bridgeport, California, is also a working ranch located at 6,500 feet in the Eastern Sierra. This historic 4,500-acre ranch was founded in 1861 by Napoleon Bonaparte Hunewill. Hunewill came to California during the gold rush, first making a stake in the area with a lumber mill business in Buckeye Canyon, which supplied wood to the boomtown of Bodie. With time, new railroads were built, which created more competition, so Hunewill made a pivotal decision to switch to cattle ranching—to supply beef to the miners in Bodie.

The next two generations of Hunewills continued cattle ranching, but the Great Depression took its toll on the business. Beef was selling for three cents a pound and they had difficulties paying their taxes. So in 1931, Lenore and Stanley Hunewill decided to offer guest accommodations at the ranch to help make ends meet. That crucial decision was beneficial, and today the historic ranch is the oldest working guest ranch in California—where guests can ride horses and help push cattle in a spectacular mountain setting.

Offering old-fashioned western hospitality, the ranch feels more like home, with many families returning year after year. With 150 well-trained mounts, the ranch has horses for every ability—from beginner level to expert. With a seasoned staff and plenty of scenic mountain trails, the ranch offers some great horseback riding along with a slate of other activities. The 4th of July is a fun-filled week that is perfect for families. For the expert riders, the Buckeye Gather is a way to truly experience the high country while driving cows back to the ranch—complete with chuck wagon meals and cowboy music.

Another unique event is the annual cattle drive that moves five hundred to eight hundred head of cattle from Bridgeport, California to the winter range in Smith Valley, Nevada. This sixty-mile, five-day drive is for intermediate and expert riders, offering a once-in-a-lifetime chance to move cattle through some beautiful red rock canyons, old historic ranches, and open rangeland with the breathtaking Sierra Nevada and Sweetwater Mountains as a backdrop. This is a real working drive where riders must be prepared to face the elements and help push the cows along the dusty trail.

Patti Williams, from Orange, California, participated in her first Hunewill drive in 2018 and shared, "I have been raised with cattle and livestock my entire life, so being around cattle was nothing new. I was finally able to go on this drive with two friends once I retired. Being on the Hunewill drive was the most amazing experience of my life. Up at the crack of dawn, working and caring for the cattle while moving them across the rangeland…I felt like I was living the history of the Old West. I was so blessed to share such an incredible experience—bringing me to tears some days."

Top: Time to move 'em out—at the start of the drive. Bottom: Starting in the Eastern Sierra, the cattle drive travels through some stunning landscapes.

On the Hunewill Cattle Drive, a chuck wagon follows the sixty-mile drive, providing hot drinks and lunch for the crew. On the historic trail drives, the chuck wagon was the center of social life for the cattle outfit. It's where the meals were prepared, where campfire stories were shared, and it carried the provisions needed for the cowhands.

Typically, cattle drives move the livestock in the fall months when the seasons are starting to change. In the Sierra Nevada, there is always a threat of snow at the higher elevations throughout the year.

Top: Every fall, five hundred to eight hundred head of cattle are moved from the summer pastures to the winter range in Smith Valley, Nevada. The locals enjoy this annual ritual, one that started over 110 years ago. Preserving a piece of California's history, this drive helps keep the spirit of the Old West alive in the Eastern Sierra.

Today the ranch is run by the siblings—Megan, Betsy, and Jeff Hunewill—along with their spouses. Their children now have an active role at the ranch, being the sixth generation to carry on the traditions handed down from previous generations. Living in God's country, the Hunewill family has done a tremendous job preserving and sharing a piece of California's history that can be enjoyed for many more generations to come.

One Too Many Aces—the western frontier was full of risk-taking speculators and miners who spent much time at the poker table. In virtually every mining camp, a poker table could be found in each saloon. *Photo Credit: Antonio Elumba and Sandy Powell.*

CHAPTER SIX

GUNFIGHTERS AND VIGILANTE JUSTICE DURING THE GOLD RUSH

The term "gunfighter" was not used until the 1880s, but the inception of the gunfighter era began in 1848 with the discovery of gold in northern California. As a result of the California Gold Rush, the largest voluntary mass migration of emigrants occurred in 1849 and 1850. This huge influx of newcomers also included gold-seekers from Mexico, Chili, Peru, the Caribbean, Europe, China, and Australia. The gold rush attracted mostly young, single males who came looking for instant wealth, along with plenty of dishonest hustlers, petty thieves, and convicts.

The California Gold Rush brought wealth to a few but most encountered disappointment, despair, and even death. Life in the mining camps was primitive, with food and supplies being scarce. The common currency for trading was gold dust carried in buckskin pouches. Crime was rare the first year of the gold rush, but by 1852 the easy pickings were far less abundant as streams were "panned out." The increased competition resulted in more robberies and murders.

In the early years of the gold rush, government was minimal, and most of the mining camps were set up in remote areas with essentially no law enforcement nor any sense of social responsibility. Each county had a sheriff, a few deputies, a justice of the peace, and a constable. The counties in the mining areas only had a small, primitive jail, and jailbreaks were common. Additionally, as thousands of immigrants from diverse religious and racial backgrounds were thrown together in mining districts, they became bold and reckless in these lawless regions, especially when fueled with alcohol, revolvers, and Bowie knives. Firearms became a necessity—one could not travel without one, nor sleep without one under the pillow. It was fully understood that life on the frontier or in mining camps involved settling one's own problems and being able to defend one's self.

"Well…did he fire five shots or six?"

"Don't be sneakin' up behind me when we're playin' poker!" —*Photo Credit: Antonio Elumba and Sandy Powell.*

The gold rush coincided with the development of the Colt revolvers—the most important being the .44-caliber Dragoon models of 1848, the .31-caliber Pocket model of 1849, and the .36-caliber Navy model of 1851, as well as the many "pepperbox" models made by Allen & Thurber.[45] These pistols had revolving cylinders or barrels allowing either five or six shots, which were a huge improvement over the single-shot weapons. These revolvers were so popular that they were brought to California by the thousands during the gold rush.

In reality, the miner's weapon of choice was the Bowie knife, because it was easily concealed and was more dependable than the revolving pistol that frequently misfired. In the 1850s the term "Bowie knife" was used to describe any type of sheath knife or butcher knife. To survive, the gold rush gunfighters had to be quite skillful with a six-shooter and the Bowie knife.

Before the legendary gunfights at the O.K. Corral in Tombstone, one of the deadliest shootouts occurred in Rocky Canyon in Placer County, California. In 1854, Jonathan R. Davis was out on foot along a miner's trail with two friends. While hiking, they were ambushed by a party of eleven outlaws who had recently robbed and murdered six Chinese men and four Americans a few days prior in the same location. As a result, one of Davis' friends was fatally shot and the other was wounded. Davis, with his exceptional shooting skills, was quick to react—pulling out both of his Colt revolvers as he fired nonstop at the charging outlaws. He shot down the outlaws one by one, leaving seven dying on the ground. The four remaining outlaws surrounded Davis with Bowie knives and a short sword. Davis quickly drew his Bowie knife, severely wounding three of them and cutting off the nose of the last one.

The shootout story was reported as a sham by the local newspapers but was later confirmed by three miners who were out hunting that day and witnessed the whole incident. This unbelievable gunfight demonstrated the dangers that miners encountered on a daily basis in the lawless Sierra Nevada.

In addition to the frequent robberies, the saloons and gambling halls in the mining towns were home to many shootouts, bar brawls, and street fights. This constant violence required lawmen with nerves of steel, which were in short supply. This brazen lawlessness resulted in the ever-popular vigilante justice, which was viewed as socially constructive in times of need.

During the gold rush, the vigilante movement was accepted with overwhelming approval. The first lynching took place in Dry Diggins, which later earned the nickname of Hangtown, and today is called Placerville. According to the journalist, Edward Gould Buffum, a Mexican gambler named Lopez was in possession of a large amount of money and was held up by five robbers. With a gun held to his head, Lopez quietly alerted others and nearby miners rushed in to capture them. The five robbers were tried by a jury chosen by the local citizens and sentenced to thirty-nine lashes each.

Afterward, three of the men were recognized as suspects in a robbery and an attempted murder case from several months earlier. Two hundred men showed up and organized themselves into a jury. The trial lasted about thirty minutes and they were left to ask themselves, "What shall be done with them?" One miner cried out, "Hang them." The three men were placed in a wagon with nooses around their necks and were promptly hung.

Throughout the mining communities, when certain crimes compromised the safety of the community, angry residents organized vigilante committees. This rough form of justice administered a variety of punishments which included: flogging, head shaving, branding, tar and feathering, or banishment from town.

Today there are a number of re-enactor gunfighter and vigilante groups that keep the spirit of the gunfighter alive throughout the Sierra Nevada: the *Nevada Gunfighters* in Carson City, Nevada, the *Horsethief Canyon Gang* in Reno, Nevada, the *Foothill Vigilantes* in Virginia City, Nevada, the *Hangtown Marshalls* in Placerville, California, and the *Sierra Nevada Guns for Hire* in Pioneer, California.

"Life is not always a matter of holding good cards, but sometimes, playing a poor hand well."

—Robert Louis Stevenson.

Trouble's brewing — The Nevada Gunfighters participate in many events in the Carson City area.

73

Bob Gillott, of the *Nevada Gunfighters*, aka "Pronto Pike"—a character from Louis L'Amour's *Hanging Woman Creek* novel—shared his thoughts about what goes into taking on a gunfighter character. "A lot of work goes into developing an authentic or fictional image as far as costuming and accoutrements, from hats to boots. Researching an actual historical character is a task that involves a lot of time to gain accurate information. Then there is 'the look.' This too is a time-consuming endeavor, which in the end is rewarding in the presentation and performance of the character."

Left: Got 'em covered. *Photo Credit: Antonio Elumba and Sandy Powell.*

Hangtown Marshals: Keeping law and order in Old Hangtown.

Left: "Aim at a high mark and you will hit it."

– Annie Oakley.

75

"Lie the scattered remnants of yesteryear, and a ghost town called Bodie sings its sad song."

—Sallie Knowles Joseph

CHAPTER SEVEN

BODIE – FROM BOOM TOWN TO BUST

Bodie is unique in its history among the ghost towns of the West. Today Bodie remains in a "state of arrested decay"—completely frozen in a moment of time when the town was abandoned in the economic downturn of the early 1900s. The Boone brothers of the Boone Store & Warehouse said, "We'll be back when times are better." Well, the good times never fully returned and, in the meantime, the old jars of beans and cans of mustard collect layers of dust, reminding us that the good times to be had in Bodie are long gone.

But as a ghost town, Bodie is the real deal. Compared to Tombstone or Virginia City, there are no commercial exploits taking front and center stage—no staged gunfights nor trinkets being hawked on the street corners. The realistic nature of the preserved ghost town is due to the state of California making it a historical park in 1962.

Gold was discovered in the Bodie area in 1859 by a group of prospectors including the namesake—W.S. Bodey. They were prospecting in Monoville and ventured into the hills of the treeless, high desert following creeks up above 8,300 feet elevation. Supposedly they uncovered a vein of gold while trying to retrieve a wounded rabbit in a hole.

News of the gold spread quickly and other prospectors joined in the hunt for gold, resulting in the establishment of a mining district. The following winter Bodey perished in a blizzard while bringing supplies back from Monoville. His body was buried in the snowdrifts and not found until the following spring.

Bodey never got to see the boomtown that emerged that bore his name. It would take another seventeen years before the rest of the world would learn that Bodie was one of the largest gold and silver deposits in California. In the years following Bodey's death, the name of the town was changed to Bodie after a careless misspelling on a sign, according to local tales.

The mining district of Bodie remained fairly quiet for seventeen years because it was overshadowed by the spectacular discoveries of silver in Aurora, Nevada and at the Comstock Lode in Virginia City, Nevada. Bodie finally boomed when the Standard Mining Company discovered a large gold deposit in 1876. And then the rush was on! During the bonanza years of 1879 through 1881, Bodie was considered one of the richest mining towns in the West, turning it into a Wild West boomtown.

The population approached 10,000 during these peak years, with over 450 businesses established. Since Bodie became a major hub, the streets became regularly congested. It was common to see large hitches pulling ore wagons, wagons filled with lumber, and numerous freight wagons—some pulled by twenty mule teams. By early 1878, daily stages were running between Bodie and Aurora, Bridgeport, and Carson City. Six-horse stagecoaches were "filled with passengers from deck to keel. Sixteen is an average load; but as a stagecoach is like a can of sardines, there is always room for just one more."[46]

Additionally, a telegraph line was built to connect Bodie with Bridgeport, California and Genoa, Nevada. There was also a Chinatown where the Chinese provided laundry services, opium dens, and cut wood brought in by burros. At one point, there were numerous gambling halls and over sixty saloons that kept the men "well-watered," while contributing to the drunken and reckless bravado. It didn't take long for Bodie to earn a reputation for being "the most lawless, wildest, and toughest mining camp the far West has ever known."[47] There was never a shortage of stagecoach robberies, shootouts, and barroom fights to keep the Wild West spirit alive.

With the sudden development of the mines in the Bodie area, there was a huge demand for lumber and cordwood. The wood was used to fuel the demanding stamp mills and provide heat to the residents' houses. Since wood was an essential commodity in the treeless community of Bodie, a local railroad was constructed in 1881 to help move timber from the nearby Mono Mills. However, the *Bodie Railway and Lumber Co.* was a local line that never connected to any outside railroad lines.

Life in Bodie was harsh and not a place for the weak. Because of the high altitude, there were very few months of frost-free weather. Blizzards were common in the winter, and at an elevation of 8,379 feet, the winter temperatures could drop to -40°F. Additionally, the winds created tall snowdrifts in town, often reaching the rooftops, making winter life a challenge. Horses and transportation were still a necessity in the winter, so the horses were equipped with crude "horse snowshoes" composed of a steel plate and fitted with a clamp to help overcome the deep snow and ice.[48]

After four short years, Bodie's boom ended. As miners began to leave in search of easier get-rich-quick mines, the population started to decline. Since the local railway never connected to an outside line, the remote location also added to the town's demise.

Top: At *Friends of Bodie Day*, there is no shortage of lawmen, scoundrels, weary miners, high-society ladies, and esteemed teamsters seen around town.

Bottom: Pack mules were used extensively in Bodie — hauling ore and supplies.

In 1881, the population dipped below 3,000, resulting in a more family-oriented community. The decline continued and the population was recorded as 698 people in 1910.[49] The Standard Consolidated Mine closed in 1913. Continuing its decline, the *San Francisco Chronicle* reported that only thirty people remained in Bodie in 1921. Then in 1932, a disastrous fire swept through town, taking with it many of the old structures. Since few people resided in the town, there was no need to rebuild.

The town of Bodie that exists today is a carryover from the Great Depression. The 230 structures that remain are the relics from the fire of 1932. In the 1940s the ghost town faced many threats of vandalism, as witnessed by many other mining towns in Nevada. James S. Cain bought up many of the town lots and mining claims when the town was in decline. Additionally, the Cain family hired caretakers to help protect the town and its structures. Today we should all be indebted to the invaluable protections that the Cain family provided in a time of dire need.

Today Bodie is a bustling ghost town—not from any mining enterprises, but from the 200,000 tourists who visit annually. Those numbers are impressive, since part of the road is unpaved and the road is closed six to seven months of the year due to winter weather.

I remember my first drive on that dirt road thirty-plus years ago—a rough drive with an endless washboard. The road starts in pinyon pine and juniper trees, climbing through green meadows that host 2,000 domestic sheep in the summer. In the early morning hours, sage grouse can be seen near the road, with a few antelope (pronghorns) off in the distance. Near the top, there are breathtaking views of the Eastern Sierra, but the trees soon disappear, and the hills become an endless sea of sagebrush. Coming around the last bend, the ghost town appears, and the valley is surrounded by a stark landscape far from any civilization, leaving one to ponder—"how did those early settlers live here in the winter?"

The dirt road is better maintained nowadays and visitors are highly rewarded for their efforts. Whether you believe in ghosts or not, the pioneer spirit of the town is still evident—with its dirt roads, wooden boardwalk, saloons, and old wooden structures that creak with the wind. The former grandeur has quietly washed away over the years, leaving dilapidated houses with peeling wallpaper, while the occasional tumbleweed dodges between the buildings. It reminds you of that opening scene in so many old Westerns—the hanging sign creaking in the wind, in an abandoned western town, with not a soul in sight.

Ore cars leaving a mine tunnel. According to old stories, there was a legendary mule named Old Tom who would pull up to six ore cars. He refused to pull the cars if he heard a seventh car being hooked up. Not only could Old Tom count, but he could also tell time. When he heard the noon whistle, he abruptly stopped working. *Photo courtesy of County of Inyo, Eastern California Museum.*

Top: Mule teams were a common sight in Bodie in the late 1800s.

Top left: Burros hauling firewood through the streets of Bodie. *Photo courtesy of the California History Room, California State Library, Sacramento, California.*

Bottom left: A doctor's buggy passing by the Dechambeau Hotel and Independent Order of Odd Fellows meeting hall.

FRIENDS OF BODIE DAY

Every year, the second Saturday in August, the ghost town of Bodie comes back to life in all its glory—like an 1880s scene from a Hollywood script. The town fills up with western characters in the appropriate period-piece clothing along with an assortment of authentic buggies, wagons, and surreys. The distinctive sounds of horses snorting along with the chorus of trace-chains jingling and iron-rimmed wheels grinding through the streets add to the soundtrack of this historic scene.

The annual *Friends of Bodie* event attracts ardent fans of the Old West who flock to the Bodie Hills to reminisce about the golden years of Bodie. Some of these western fans spend months preparing their outfits for their customary annual appearance—like a debutante making her first debut into society. If some of the bystanders witnessed the amount of work put into their outfits, they might call them a bunch of crazed fashionistas.

These western characters come to life through their costumes along with their stories. Portraying an old character from the West helps keep the spirit of the Old West alive—a part of history that never stops fascinating us. The western frontier was vast, undeveloped, and free from law and order. It was truly wild. The larger-than-life characters who ruled the West took full advantage of its lawlessness. Gambling, shootouts, highway robbery, and heavy drinking were a way of life for the most famous of the outlaws. And Bodie had its share of outlaws and unruly behavior.

So it is very fitting that the *Friends of Bodie* event helps bring these larger-than-life characters back to life. It is common to see defenders of the law coupled with foul-mouthed outlaws. And there is no shortage of scoundrels, famous bandits, well-to-do entrepreneurs, weary miners, esteemed teamsters, hard-working Chinamen, ambitious saloon keepers, high-society ladies, fugitives wanted in other parts, and even some famous madams of the nearby Red Light District. Walking through town, you might get a chance to hear one of these re-enactors share one of their tall tales of the famous characters that once roamed the streets of Bodie back in its heyday.

To complement the legendary characters who walk the streets, the event is teeming with many historic wagons pulled by teams of horses or mules, guided by the steady hand of the mighty teamster.

You'll also find many outriders on their trusty steeds, with their heads held high for all to admire. And occasionally you might see a saddle-mule as a gentle reminder to some that Kit Carson treasured his mules—riding them high up on the narrow trails of the Sierra Nevada. And one year, an 1896 Hearse made an appearance helping to carry the "bones of Bodey" through town in a funeral procession, to honor the namesake of Bodie.

Out for a stroll in the Bodie Hills.

Ardent fans of the Old West reminisce about the golden years of Bodie. Some participants spend months making and preparing their clothing ensembles for their annual appearance at *Friends of Bodie Day*. Pictured are custom-made, period outfits complete with a handmade bustle.

There is no place like Bodie—a special ghost town preserved and tucked away on the California-Nevada border. Wendy Bailey, one of the teamsters at *Friends of Bodie Day*, sums up her experiences at Bodie: "Driving down the narrow, dirt streets of Bodie along with the smell of sage and the jingle of the trace chains brings to heart a sheer joy. The reflections of your wagon in the weathered general store's hand-blown windows never fails to transport you back to the days of old. Deep emotions well up as you wipe a tear from your eye. You leave with a deep sense of respect and gratitude for the generations that walked the streets before us."

A mule pack string hauling supplies with the Standard Stamp Mill in the background.

Top: At *Friends of Bodie Day*, you'll find many outriders on their trusty steeds, some of which have very long ears.

Top left: The *Living History Ladies* enjoy an outing in Bodie, wearing handmade bustle dresses that were common in the 1870s to 1880s.

Bottom left: The *Friends of Bodie* event is teeming with many historic wagons pulled by teams of horses or mules, guided by the steady hands of the mighty teamsters.

Bodie

Across the lava and sagebrush covered hills,
Where the cold wind's voice is shrill and strong,
Lie the scattered remnants of yesteryear,
And a ghost town called Bodie sings its sad song.

Gold beckoned them here by the thousands,
And greed nourished every weary bone,
Their hearts became calloused, just like their hands—
Soon they would reap what they had sown.

The harsh winters brought them pneumonia,
And the hot summers only grief and despair.
But the promise of fortune kept them steadfast,
Until they shunned common sense, without care.

Firewater and whiskey fed their thirsty souls,
And bullets took more lives than age…
When glitter disappeared and the boom went bust,
More than tears began to fall on the sage.

Those who could leave, left in droves,
Taking what they could carry on their backs,
Anywhere else would be better than here,
And they left behind only desperate tracks.

The cemetery tells it in writing,
Of countless lives lost of both young and old.
Ghosts haunt all of what remains with regret,
Since tombstones only mark a few stories told.

Mother Nature groans with sweet revenge,
As the sun darts frivolously on the sand.
Playing peek-a-boo through the breaks in the clouds—
Now only shadows dance here in Bodie Land.

© Sallie Knowles Joseph

A moment in time.

An 1896 S&S horse-drawn hearse parked in front of the Methodist Church, built in 1882.

84

Reflecting on the road to town.

Unlike the Swazey Hotel, which is in a "state of arrested decay," this beautifully restored Peter Schuttler grain wagon, circa 1880s, is proudly driven through the streets of Bodie.

There is no shortage of saddle mules at the *Friends of Bodie* event.

The mule is the unsung hero of the equine world: It helped build the West, worked in underground mines, pulled large payloads of borax through the desert, and helped build and maintain trails in the backcountry.

CHAPTER EIGHT

THE MULE

When treated with patience, kindness, and respect, mules can be as capable as horses in all kinds of equine activities. Mules CAN DO!

—Meredith Hodges, American equine trainer and educator.

The mule is the hybrid offspring of a male donkey (a jack) and a female horse (a mare). Like most hybrids, mules are for the most part sterile. The horse passed on her athletic ability while the donkey passed on his intelligence, smaller hooves, long ears, a better range of vision, and hardiness in harsh, dry conditions. On first inspection, mules resemble a horse in height but have a shorter, wider neck, long ears, a thick mane, thinner legs, and smaller hooves. Horses evolved on the plains and learned to outrun predators and perceived threats. In contrast, donkeys evolved in the desert or arid mountains, causing them to evaluate a threat before fleeing. Was it safer for him to run off a cliff or stand his ground and evaluate the situation?

This combination of horse and donkey resulted in a remarkable animal—an animal that is intelligent, sure-footed, hardy, and long-lived. The mule also inherited the self-preservation traits of the donkey and will consider the situation before making a decision. This trait has gotten the mule mislabeled as "stubborn" and "not smart." Nothing could be further from the truth!

Mules come in a variety of sizes, colors, and types. In the 1800s, mules were "working mules" and classified by their size and use: mining mules, farm mules, sugar mules, cotton mules, and draft mules. Draft mules were favored over draft horses in the second half of the nineteenth century because they gained a reputation of being hardy and having better self-preservation.

In the 1850s, mules were highly regarded for their endurance and hardiness since they survived the harrowing journey to California in mass wagon trains, in better numbers than the teams of oxen or horses. And it was the "one-eyed mule" that helped save the Death Valley '49ers who got lost in the desert, narrowly escaping their deadly journey. William Lewis Manly and John Rogers were sent to find an escape route and return with horses and food. After walking 250 grueling miles through the harsh desert and over many mountain passes, they reached present-day Santa Clarita and purchased two horses and a "one-eyed mule." The horses died on the arduous trip back to Death Valley but the famous one-eyed mule not only survived but helped the '49ers escape the valley. Another testament to the hardiness of the mule.

Mules were preferred by pioneers, soldiers, scouts, and mountain men in the difficult and uncharted terrain of the frontier. Kit Carson—remembered as a rifle-toting hero among the celebrated mountain men—preferred a saddle mule over a horse. The surefootedness of the mule enabled the mountain men to travel higher up rocky, narrow trails in the mountains.

The surefootedness of the mule is still appreciated in modern times. Kit Branch, who has received many accolades at Bishop Mule Days, shared her story about being converted to a mule rider. "Many years ago, I was visiting my cousin in Montana, who asked if I wanted to ride a mule. Not having ridden a mule before, I thought, 'How different can it be from riding a horse?' I got an education that day. My cousin led us way, way up the mountain, upon no trail or solid footing, to a place I would have never ridden my horse. That mule never missed a step, and I became hooked on this 4WD version of equine."

Mules have a businesslike attitude and notice everything around them. But mules are also very loving and affectionate—a trait inherited from the donkey. The donkey is known to develop strong bonds and "love you like a dog." I have been out in the field many times, with a large group of mules and horses. And it is always the mules that instantly come over to greet me—curious and happy to make a friend. And on more than one occasion, I have had one mule instantly bond with me, letting the other equine know that he or she has "dibs on me."

Opposite: Mules are incredible work animals. Pictured here, Kate and Judy are eager to make the journey through Death Valley on the Death Valley Wagon Drive.

Mule string waiting to be loaded.

CHAPTER NINE

MULE PACKING IN THE SIERRA NEVADA

Descendants of the pioneer, the mountain man, the cowboy, and the teamster, High Sierra packers are a breed of their own. They are men and women who have chosen to forego the comforts of civilization and embrace the simplicity of the wilderness.

—Louise A. Jackson, Author of *Mule Men*

As the frontier exploration expanded into California in the early 1800s, mountain men relied on the surefooted mule to help them explore and cross the treacherous Sierra Nevada. Kit Carson, Osborne Russell, and Joe Meek were known to ride saddle mules, while many of the mountain men used pack mules to haul their supplies into the mountains. Likewise, the early geological explorations into the Sierra Nevada relied heavily on mule transport, with Josiah Whitney and Clarence King being the most renowned explorers who depended on mules.

The mule was also a valuable commodity for the gold miners who first settled in the foothills of the Sierra Nevada. Mules were used to haul in supplies to the remote mining camps, deliver mail in the Sierra Nevada, pulverize ore by rotating the primitive Mexican Arrastra, work in the underground mines such as the Empire mine, and transport gold to the banks. It was even rumored that a four-hundred-pound printing press was hauled into a mining settlement by mules. By 1855, the California mule population had exploded to over 31,000 mules, and mule-packing became a big business in the Sierra.[50]

But mule-packing was a demanding job that required many skills. Balancing the loads was a critical aspect; if not done correctly, the mule and cargo could end up at the bottom of a steep canyon. Packing a load onto a mule requires a methodical approach while incorporating an art form in the balancing act—skills that are passed down from one generation to the next.

As the West has been tamed and developed over the last 150 years, many of the packing demands have gone by the wayside. But the pack mule has lived on—to take on new tasks—backcountry trail and dam maintenance, search and rescue operations, and recreational packing in the Sierra. With more than a hundred peaks over 13,000 feet in elevation, many parts of the four-hundred-mile long Sierra Nevada range are quite inaccessible.[51] Additionally, there are few paved roads that cross the southern Sierra, and many of the highway-crossings are closed in the winter south of Carson City, Nevada.

When the Wilderness Act came into effect in 1964, it curtailed the use of motorized vehicles and machinery in the wilderness areas. As a result, mules have been utilized to haul in bridge and dam supplies into the remote parts of the Sierra, including timbers, wheelbarrows, cement, plywood, and many other supplies. Some of the old-time packers were innovative in getting large and awkward items into the backcountry. Hauling ten- to twelve-foot-long timbers was achieved by tying two timbers on the sides of two mules in tandem.

Today, if you hike on any of the trails in the backcountry, a mule helped with the construction and maintenance of the trail. Regular trail maintenance is performed by trails crews that live in the backcountry during summer. These crews depend on mules to haul in their camp gear, food provisions, and trail tools. Additionally, the pack stations and the Backcountry Horsemen of California help repair trails in the late spring, after winter storms and water-runoff have severely damaged the trails while using mules to haul in tools.

RECREATIONAL PACKING

In the early 1900s, the Sierra Nevada was a distant novelty unknown to most folks. William Colby, the first secretary of the Sierra Club, organized many pack trips into the Sierra from 1901 to 1929 to

Packers descending the rocky Mount Whitney Trail in the early 1900s. *Photo courtesy of County of Inyo, Eastern California Museum.*

Mules typically carry 100-150 pounds of gear.

William Colby, the first secretary of the Sierra Club, organized many pack trips into the Sierra from 1901 to 1929. The Sierra Club pack trains were known to haul in thousands of pounds of gear and provisions, including canoes. Circa: 1925. *Photo courtesy of the California History Room, California State Library, Sacramento, California.*

help people experience the backcountry firsthand. In 1903, there was a Sierra Club trip to Mount Whitney provided by the Broder & Hopping outfit. The pack train consisted of eighty-five mules and saddle animals and 30,000 pounds of baggage, camp equipment, and provisions. The cost of the five-week trip was $5 for each participant.[52]

Today recreational-packing is not quite as ambitious as those early packers from a century ago. The Sierra Nevada has pack stations and outfitters located on the east and west sides, offering a variety of pack trips that can be customized to your needs. A "spot" or dunnage trip enables you to hike or ride in with your gear packed in by mule. Your provisions are dropped off at your destination or base camp and picked up at a later date for your return trip out of the backcountry. These trips are also ideal for backpackers who want to cover more mileage in the backcountry with less effort.

For those who want to enjoy the most incredible wilderness vacation, a full-service pack trip is the ticket. These trips provide freshly cooked meals, camp gear, and a gentle trail horse to ride. Just leave it to the camp-cook and packers who will haul in your personal gear plus tents, group toilets, chairs, stoves, dutch ovens, solar showers, and lanterns.

Mules are used to carry challenging items into the backcountry. Pictured is a fourteen-foot-long screw-rod used to open a gate, nestled between two timbers. Rick Edney built a couple of platforms to sit on the sawbuck pack-saddles while also incorporating a swivel device and a cradle made out of horseshoes. The mules had to learn to work in tandem around the trail switchbacks, with the lead mule traveling almost 180 degrees to the second mule. *Photo Credit: Rick Edney.*

Pack mules have been used to haul gear into and out of the Sierra Nevada for the last 170 years.

As an active backpacker in my 20s, I enjoyed hauling around my forty-five-pound backpack, sleeping on the hard ground, and wearing the same filthy clothes for a week. But I could never get excited about the crappy, overly salty, diarrhea-inducing, freeze-dried food choices. As I've gotten older, I've come to appreciate having a meal prepared with fresh food, a chair to recline in around the campfire while sipping some cold beer or wine, and having a puffy pillow to help me sleep better at night. Hiring a pack outfit is the finest way to explore the backcountry of the High Sierra!

Wilderness pack trips offer an unforgettable adventure into the unspoiled backcountry, crossing trails that were once used by early mountain men and gold-seekers when the state was being explored and settled. After cresting a 10,000-foot granite mountain pass, you will witness lakes in every imaginable color of blue and teal, lush meadows, and dramatic rainbow-hued ridges. Once you reach sensory overload, the compass of your soul will be drawn there forever.

"The trail is the thing, not the end of the trail. Travel too fast, and you miss all you are traveling for."

—Louis L'Amour

Pack trips are a great way to escape the city and get into the backcountry.

The Sierra Nevada is diverse in its geology and landscape, providing a backdrop for many stunning images.

McGee Creek–The Packer's Song

Into the canyon with the trail far below,
Down to the pinons where the sweetwater flows,
Back stream behind me in the yellowing light,
Onto the meadow where we wait for night.

Mountains in shadow, silver with age,
Moonlight on aspens, granite and sage,
Horses graze lonesome where the outlet pours down,
I roll out my blankets and I sleep on the ground.

Ride, ride, ride on through time,
Far off the cities, their whistling whine,
Dream like, these hoofbeats, dream-like this song,
Dream like this lifetime, as I ride along.

Gray mist at dawning, seen from the black,
Listen for the bell mare, diamond the packs.
Shiver near the campfire and wait for the sun,
Red glow of the morning and a new day has begun.

Ride, ride, ride on through time,
Far off the cities, their whistling whine,
Dream like, these hoofbeats, dream-like this song,
Dream like this lifetime, as I ride along.

© Copyright Dave Stamey.

Dave Stamey spent several summers in the High Sierra working as a packer and guide for McGee Creek Pack Station. His years at McGee Creek inspired many of his treasured songs about the Sierra Nevada. Lee Roeser shared that Stamey is a great storyteller and he used to sing around the campfire, entertaining the guests on the horse drives. Stamey has been voted seven times *Entertainer of the Year* and five times *Songwriter of the Year* by the Western Music Association. His songs capture the spirit of the modern cowboy in a world of rapid flux—reminding us that in the western world, some things never change.

The fall colors are spectacular in McGee Creek Canyon.

Size is relative. This mule string is making its way up to the saddle—providing a relative scale of size in this valley of the majestic Eastern Sierra.

"Yesterday's trails are now worn deep into my soul...
The details are forever ingrained on and in my heart.
I retravel all these paths and recover their wonders,
In the high country where all good memories start."

— Sallie Knowles Joseph

Stunning views and vistas near Laurel Pass in the Eastern Sierra—McGee Creek Pack Station.

The Self-Reliant Packer

As a kid, John Summers spent most of his summers up in the high country at Mammoth Lakes Pack Outfit, which was owned by his dad, Lee Summers. Kids back in those days learned at an early age how to help out at the ranch or pack station. Besides attending to the endless manure detail, John Summers learned valuable roping and packing techniques from the pack station and their family cattle operation. He spent many hours on horseback in the backcountry with his dad learning important skills that would carry him forward in life as a packer.

One summer in the late 1950s, one of the outfit's packers had the misfortune of pulling his thumb off in the backcountry while hosting a large party of clients. Known to be self-reliant, the packers had a system to notify the pack station if they needed help in the backcountry. There were no cellphones or other means of communication back then. So they took the bridle off one of the horses and tied up the stirrups—as a message to the pack station—and sent the horse down the trail. Horses and mules know the way home quite well, but tying up the stirrups was a way to let the pack station know that the horse was purposely sent back. An SOS message!

Back at the pack station, Lee Summers received the SOS message and made preparations for some sort of rescue in the backcountry, without knowing all the details. With limited packers available that day, Summers brought along John in case he needed an extra hand, but it would also be a good way to spend some quality time together. John was only eight years old but was quite adept at handling the stock. They had to travel twenty to twenty-five miles one way to get to the packer at Lost Keys Lake—a long and difficult journey with three tough climbs.

After spending the night, Lee would take care of evacuating the packer but had to divvy up the other responsibilities of getting the mules and clients out of the backcountry. He had a string of five mules that needed to be led out on the arduous journey back to the pack station. Short on help, John was given the task to bring the pack string, fully loaded, out on his own. Ask any packer, and this is a task that normally requires a seasoned stock handler. John not only expertly handled the mule string, but he put in forty to fifty miles for the two-day venture. This mileage alone was an extraordinary feat, but his fearless determination and remarkable skill set, at the tender age of eight, helped his dad overcome the challenges of the rescue.

Today John Summers, owner of the Mammoth Lakes Pack Outfit, passes down the valuable skills he learned from his dad to the next generation of packers. He is a third-generation packer and comes from a top pedigree of packers—his grandfather, Lloyd Summers, was one of the early packers in the Owens Valley area, starting the pack station in 1915. John's son, Jared Summers, is the fourth generation to carry forward the traditions and skills passed down from a century ago.

String of Diamonds

Sometimes the search for fame and fortune
Destiny nags at the heart in a vanishing voice.
Along the way there are numerous tempting forks
Into the unknown there's always a choice.

The horse's bridle reflects a glint of silver
Light brown hair is sun-streaked with gold.
Some riches are often underestimated
To the treasure tethered in a hand to hold.

As it should be, all things rely on balance
Between looking ahead and looking back.
Ahead lie the decisions, behind the lessons learned
Focusing on the tension, always adjusting the slack.
Leather fringe swings freely in the Sierra breeze
Stirring the mind, searching destiny's plan.
Some tarnish their lives in search for Nirvana
Instead of finding solace in what's in their hand.

Unlike a string of pearls whose likeness adds value,
Diamonds are all different in carats, clarity, and size.
Some diamonds are set tightly with lash ropes and leather,
A uniqueness only the holder can realize.

Maneuvering through life like a vagabond gypsy,
The rope dancer grips tightly to what money can't buy.
Taking stock in the rough-cut journey toward the horizon,
Making tracks to where the mountains meet the sky—

Through switchbacks, storms, and rocky trails—
There's an awareness of the connection to the land.
Facets reveal memories and dreams to come—
All through the string of diamonds in their hand.

Mules relay trust and honesty with each sure-footed step,
With guidance from above, in perfect symmetry

The trail of life through the High Country is in unison—
With a String of Diamonds—a packers Rosary……

(This poem makes references to diamond hitches—a lashing technique used to tie or secure a load onto a pack animal.)

© Sallie Knowles Joseph

Mules Aid in Search-and-Rescue Efforts

Mules have been used for search-and-rescue operations in the backcountry for generations. As helicopters have become more powerful and available over the years, they have evacuated more of the traumatic injuries in the backcountry. But lesser injuries are still evacuated by mules and horses.

In the 1960s and '70s, helicopter rescues in the backcountry were not common since they were very costly, few helicopters were available, and most helicopters were not powerful enough to fly to higher altitudes (the military helicopters were the best suited). So mules and horses were heavily relied on for rescues in those days.

In 1972, there was a woman backpacker who had been traveling by herself in the Sierra Nevada for almost two weeks. She was found collapsed on the trail near Purple Lake by other backpackers, who hiked out and notified Lou and Marye Roeser—current owners of Mammoth Lakes Pack Outfit at the time. It was a busy day at the pack station, with many pack strings already on the trail. No extra wranglers were available.

So Lou Roeser rode in with an extra saddle horse and mule to check on the backpacker, knowing full well that she might have to be evacuated. It was a long and challenging ten-mile trip into Purple Lake—about four hours one way. The trail starts at 8,900 feet, then climbs and descends the arduous switchbacks over Duck Pass (almost 11,000 feet), which offers magnificent views of Fish Creek Basin, leaving one more climb through the steep "rock-chute" into Purple Lake. He found the woman in bad shape and she was in no condition to ride a horse. It appeared that she needed some oxygen, so Roeser rode the ten miles back out. Once he made it back to the pack station, he notified the US Forest Service and the sheriff to see

A McGee Creek packer leads a string of mules into the John Muir Wilderness of California's Eastern Sierra Nevada.

if they could hunt down a helicopter that might be available for a high-altitude evacuation. At this point, the sun was starting to set, and a helicopter evacuation was out of the question.

Not wanting to sit around and wait, Roeser acquired some oxygen along with some blankets and other supplies for the woman. He made a second trip back to the Purple Lake area to check on the woman, bringing an extra saddle horse and supplies on a mule. As the darkness set in, he put his blind faith in his trusty steed—since horses and mules are known to have good night vision. Settling into a slow and steady pace, Roeser and his animals traveled into the night, finally reaching the woman. She was breathing better but still not able to ride out. So a helicopter would need to evacuate her if one were available.

Roeser then turned around and made the long haul back on the treacherous trail in the dark. He arrived at the pack station shortly after daybreak and notified the sheriff of the best location to land a helicopter if one was available. Thankfully a helicopter was available, and the woman was safely evacuated. After all was said and done, Roeser and his animals put in forty grueling miles on the High Sierra trail. The altitude alone was difficult, but add all the grueling climbs and nighttime riding and you can see why this should serve as a bleak reminder that many other early explorers in the Sierra were not so lucky.

This second-generation packer has been packing in the Eastern Sierra for almost fifty years. Packing into the backcountry requires being prepared for all types of weather and the unexpected.

A sheepherder watches over his band of sheep from above, with the Eastern Sierra Nevada in the background.

CHAPTER TEN

BASQUE SHEEPHERDING IN THE SIERRA NEVADA

The first Basque to arrive in California followed the Gold Rush of 1849. Since most did not find fortune in gold, many turned to sheep and cattle ranching—supplying meat and wool to the miners. By the 1880s, they expanded and moved throughout the Great Basin seeking cheaper rangeland. But a large population remained in Kern County, California raising sheep, farming grain, and growing grapes.

The Basque come from the Pyrenees Mountains straddling the French and Spanish border and are known to be fiercely independent. Coming from a "land-starved country," they recognized the vast open rangeland in the West as a huge opportunity. As more Basque immigrated to the western states, they could easily find work as a sheepherder since the job does not require being proficient with the English language nor any formal training. Additionally, if they worked hard, they could acquire their own band of sheep within a few years. In lieu of wages, many of the herders were paid off in sheep stock and eventually branched off on their own. By the 1870s the sheep population had peaked to almost 6.4 million in the state of California.[53]

As word of the abounding successes in the states returned to the Basque homeland, many more dreamed of becoming "sheep rangers" in the American West. But it would still take hard work and many sacrifices to be successful. Robert Laxalt, son of Basque immigrants, eloquently described their occupation as the "lonely sentinels of the American West." The first year for the immigrants was the hardest. Jean Belleau left France in 1947 at the age of 21

and shared, "I felt the hardest thing for me was the loneliness I felt the first year."[54] Arriving in a new country without knowing the language or any of the customs, they were sent to the high country with a large band of sheep—equipped with only a tent, bedroll, and a pack burro for the summer. These dependable herders, only accompanied by their dogs, did not succumb to the extreme isolation that would have made most men go crazy.

With all their free time in the high country, many of the herders passed the time by making aspen carvings, also known as "arborglyphs." These carvings can depict artwork or crude caricatures but many document the date and hometown of the herder. Thousands of these Basque carvings have been found throughout the West, and have historical significance.

To make use of the summer grazing, the sheep were moved with the seasons. The sheep spent their winters in the lower deserts that were mostly void of snow. In the warmer months, the sheep were moved to the high country of the Sierra Nevada—where grass and water were plentiful.

In the early days, the trip to the Sierra Nevada was exhausting and demanding. Up until the 1980s, the sheep were "trailed" up, on foot, from Mojave or Bakersfield every spring to Bishop or the Mono Lake area and returned via the same route in the fall. During this era, more than 60,000 sheep were moved up in the Eastern Sierra every spring, but the herders still found pleasure in their duties.[55] Miguel Iturriria immigrated to Bakersfield in 1952 and shared his experiences on the trail:

Many people look forward to seeing the sheep at Little Round Valley, along Highway 395, in the fall. It is an annual ritual in the Eastern Sierra.

These sheep are being moved to their spring pastures, before heading up into the high country.

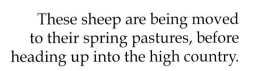

Many of the herders passed the time by making aspen carvings—known as "arborglyphs." These carvings can depict artwork or crude caricatures but many document the date and hometown of the herder. This arborglyph depicts a date of 1916.

Every spring we walked from Mojave to Mono Lake trailing the sheep on foot. The trip took forty days. Even during the tough moments we always enjoyed the trip and were so happy to reach Mono Lake. There was always plenty of time to dream of good things and reminisce about family and friends in the Old Country.[56]

But if that trip sounds daring, Paco Iturriria—who also arrived in 1952 with his brother Miguel—shared that the old-timers in the late 1800s used to trail the sheep back to Bakersfield over the Sierra Nevada. From 1865 to 1905, a series of circuitous, seasonal trails were developed over the precarious Sierra Nevada. Depending on the route, this circuitous trip would range from five hundred to seven hundred miles in total length.

These early herders moved the sheep bands through Owens Valley and up into higher mountains and meadows as they became free of snow. Continuing to the west side of the Sierra Nevada, the herders would make the journey over the steep mountain passes. These herders used several passes, including Tioga, Sonora, Ebbetts, and Carson Pass—always with a chance of an unpredictable snowstorm.[57] But times have changed, and many of the bands of sheep are now trucked in modern livestock trailers to the high country.

In the Sierra Nevada, there is a threat of snow at higher elevations throughout the year, even in the summer. One year in Bodie Hills, Paco Iturriria shared that his sheep got trapped in a snowstorm. It dumped more than two feet of snow, so the herders had to dig a trail for the sheep to get down to a lower elevation. They feared that they might have lost some, but surprisingly, all the sheep made their way out.

As the economic situation in the Basque region improved in the 1970s, immigration to the states decreased. Since then, many of the herders have been recruited from Peru or Chili—working on an H-2A guest-worker permit. And with grazing permits curtailed over the years, the sheep industry has declined in recent decades in California. Additionally, the younger generation is not following in their parents' footsteps in the sheep industry since they are finding other professions to pursue.

But there is still reason to celebrate the sheep of the Sierra Nevada. In fact, the sheep are now being recognized as "four-footed fire suppression units." Outside of Carson City and Reno, Nevada,

the sheep have been used in recent years to help reduce wildfire hazards in the outlying areas in the spring. Working with city, state, and federal agencies, Borda Land & Sheep Co. of Gardnerville, Nevada sends out about 2,000 sheep and lambs to help graze the invasive cheatgrass that has altered the ecosystem and created more fire potential.

In recent years, there have been studies that found more invasive plants in non-grazed areas. These invasive species result in larger, hotter, and faster-moving fires. Cattle grazing is also beneficial, but sheep are known to be consummate grazers that can be guided in steep terrain to graze in targeted areas. With wildfires becoming more destructive in recent years, the sheep can be an efficient tool in the upcoming century as a means of prevention.

Above: French sheepherder, Pete Giraud, with his flock of 5000 sheep in Monache Meadows in 1897. Joe Eyraud is holding the goat. *Photo courtesy of County of Inyo, Eastern California Museum.*

Opposite, top left: These sheep have their full woolies during the winter.

Opposite, bottom left: Moving a band of sheep to their spring pasture.

Opposite, top right: The sheep are moved to different meadows throughout the summer season.

Opposite, bottom right: A black sheep can be seen in this photo. Patti Novak-Echenique shared, "The black ewes are 'markers' and most sheep companies put in one black sheep for every one hundred head of sheep. You can count your black sheep to see if any sheep are missing—it is a way to keep track of your sheep on the open range."

Left: Sheepherders trailing the sheep up from Mojave with the Eastern Sierra in the background. *Photo courtesy of County of Inyo, Eastern California Museum.*

Traffic jam in the Eastern Sierra.

Passing through the Alabama Hills, the caravan of one hundred mules pays homage to the water resources of California. *Photo Credit: Lou Roeser.*

CHAPTER ELEVEN

ONE HUNDRED MULES WALKING THE LOS ANGELES AQUEDUCT

In 2013 Jen and Lee Roeser, owners of McGee Creek Pack Station, were approached by the artist, Lauren Bon, to take on an enormous project—honoring the contribution of mules in the construction of the Los Angeles Aqueduct in the early 1900s—in a moving art project. Bon and her Metabolic Studio company had a vision of a cross-country art exhibition moving from Owens Valley, in the Eastern Sierra, to Los Angeles coinciding with the one hundredth anniversary of the Los Angeles Aqueduct—to be called the *One Hundred Mules Walking the Los Angeles Aqueduct.*

The art project would become a month-long meditative activity focusing on water-source awareness and the heroic efforts of mules building the West. Mules are a hybrid animal—a cross between a horse and donkey—resulting in an equine that is more sure-footed, tolerates heat better, requires less water, and in general is hardier than a horse. Since mules were the powerful workforce behind the construction of the aqueduct, a caravan of one hundred mules would help celebrate their incredible contributions to the aqueduct.

In 1908, the controversial aqueduct construction began and was overseen by William Mulholland, the chief engineer. The project would divert and deliver water from the Owens River, where the water source originates high in the Eastern Sierra Nevada, to the growing metropolis of Los Angeles. Taking five years to complete, the 270-mile aqueduct is an unlined canal that uses only gravity to move the water and generate electricity along the route. The construction of the canal required more than one million barrels of concrete, six million pounds of dynamite, the loss of forty-three construction-worker lives, and 142 tunnels to complete the project.[58] The aqueduct was completed on November 5th of 1913 and dramatically changed the Owens Valley landscape forever, while impacting future generations.

The water from the Eastern Sierra allowed the city of Los Angeles to grow from sixty-one square miles to 440 square miles in the 1920s, now supporting a population of more than four-million residents today.[59] In the 1930s, the aqueduct was extended another 150 miles to include the runoff from the Mono Lake Basin. The One Hundred Mule Aqueduct Project was a way to connect the people of Los Angeles to their water supply in the Eastern Sierra. "Many people in L.A. don't know their water comes from 270 miles away," Lauren Bon stated.

The art project was a huge undertaking, with much more involved than just rounding up one hundred mules for the project. Bon scouted and finalized the entire 270-mile route—not a minor task. Additionally, the ride involved a crew of thirty-five people, including one wrangler for each string of five to ten mules. Other tasks included: scouting and setting up eighteen campsites, getting permits from the various government agencies, devising a corral system, renting trucks, privies, and showers, providing water sources for the entire route, arranging for law-enforcement presence and escorts at fifty locations, and hiring a crew of wranglers, drivers, and cooks. Additionally, Bon organized many public events and press releases along the route. With only a few months to prepare for the event, it was an incredible feat accomplished by Bon and the Roesers.

The caravan of one hundred mules and wranglers on a ridge with the city of Los Angeles in the background. The focus of this month-long art project was to bring awareness about the water source for the city of Los Angeles and the heroic efforts of the mules who helped build the aqueduct. *Photo courtesy of Lauren Bon and The Metabolic Studio, 2013.*

On the 18th of October in 2013, the mule ride started at the actual aqueduct intake near Independence, California, embarking on a twenty-five day journey following the canal and ending at the Los Angeles Equestrian Center on Veterans Day—a total of 270 miles. Among the one hundred mules, there was a "solar" mule leading the mules, named Dolly. Dolly was equipped with solar panels and various hard drives with four different cameras documenting the 270-mile trek; she had one camera on her head, her left side, her right side, and on her haunch. And the sound of the journey was recorded by Babe, known as the "sonic" mule. The video documentation of the journey was used by Bon to make a feature documentary titled, *One Hundred Mules Walking the Los Angeles Aqueduct*, and was shown at many film festivals around the world receiving much praise.

The route passed through the Alabama Hills, and riders pointed out movie locations of films such as *Mule Train* with Gene Autry. With Mount Whitney in the background, it was hard not to be in awe of this location that has hosted many movie sets. Along the route, Bon organized many different community events to help celebrate the *One Hundred Mules Walking the Los Angeles Aqueduct* and bring to fruition one of her other goals—bringing people and communities together.

Left: A fifty-two-mule team hauling a section of steel siphon to Jawbone Canyon. Each pipe was seven and one-half feet in diameter, thirty-six feet long, and weighed twenty-six tons. *Photo courtesy of County of Inyo, Eastern California Museum.*

Right: The Los Angeles aqueduct could not have been built without the enormous contributions of mules. *Photo courtesy of County of Inyo, Eastern California Museum.*

While much has been written about this historical event, it must have been a sight to behold in the high desert of the Eastern Sierra—one hundred mules strung out over a half-mile. During the climactic descent into Los Angeles, the wranglers and mules could sense the energy and excitement that had been building up along the route. The crowds of onlookers and reporters were getting larger and larger near the end of their journey.

During the final part of the journey, the mules were decorated with American flags to honor the veterans who valiantly served in the armed forces—with the last day of the trip coinciding with Veteran's Day. It was also a day to honor the mule, the champion of the labor force that built the aqueduct. The pageantry of one hundred decorated-mules on the last leg of this momentous event was a cause for celebration.

When they reached the Los Angeles Equestrian Center, a presentation was made, then the saddles and gear were removed from the mules. The mules were slowly let loose in the arena—a reward for their steadfast efforts on the month-long trek. After twenty mules were released, the excitement slowly escalated. Once all the animals were loose, it was "mule euphoria"—with all the mules running in circles around the arena, including a few on the sidelines rolling around in the dirt.

Jen Roeser summed up the rewarding and ambitious journey: "The One Hundred Mule Ride was not only the adventure of a lifetime, but it gave me the opportunity to work with a visionary artist to bring remembrance to a unique part of history that should never be forgotten. Having the opportunity to showcase the unsung hero of the story, the American mule, was the fulfillment of the mission, and frosting on the cake!"

Just as the aqueduct construction project was a huge and innovative undertaking in 1908, Lauren Bon's project was an equally difficult and innovative project which tried to highlight this ongoing tug-of-war for water in the state of California. Hopefully, there is a new awareness about the sources of city water in a state that will now have to contend with ongoing drought conditions, global warming, and extreme fire conditions in the next century.

Kudos to Lauren Bon, the Roesers, the wranglers, and the magnificent mules for their tireless efforts to make this grand vision a reality.

Owens Valley

The Owens Valley was known for its farming and ranching operations in the early 1900s, but it has been a target of deceptive tactics to obtain water rights since the 1920s, when the California Water Wars erupted and resulted in the Owens Valley under the power of Los Angeles Department of Water and Power (LADWP). Over the years, a series of lawsuits have been leveraged against LADWP when the water withdrawals affected the region's fish, bird, and wildlife habitat of the Eastern Sierra and Mono Lake. As a result, water withdrawals must be managed to keep the water level of Mono Lake, in the Eastern Sierra, at a minimum of 6,391 feet above sea level.

Today the dry lakebed of Owens Lake, south of Lone Pine in the Eastern Sierra, is a stark reminder of the ill-effects of the aqueduct's effect on the Owens Valley region. Before the aqueduct, Owens Lake received its water from the Owens River. It held water until 1913—the year the lake water was slowly diverted to the Los Angeles Aqueduct. It's hard to believe, but the former 110-square-mile lake was once bustling. In the 1870s, the lake hosted a steamship, the *Bessie Brady*. The steamship was used to haul silver and lead bullion from the furnaces at nearby Cerro Gordo, to wagon teams on the other side of the lake. At one point, there were more than fifty wagon teams on the south end of the lake to keep up with the bullion shipments from the mine.[60] Sitting below the snow-capped Mount Whitney, the blue lake finally dried up in the 1920s, becoming a dry salt-flat which today causes disruptive dust storms for the local residents.

USFS packers bring in
supplies to a trail crew in the
backcountry in Stanislaus
National Forest.

CHAPTER TWELVE

USFS PACK MULES: MULES HELP AID FIRE CREWS IN CALIFORNIA

In remote parts of California, the steady-paced mule is a godsend to firefighters. When the US Forest Service (USFS) was established in 1905, pack animals were widely used in their operations—exploring their districts, backcountry patrol, trail maintenance, bridge building, fish stocking, and snow surveys. The US Forest Service's Region 5, which includes all the forests in California, had more than one hundred packers and approximately 2,000 head of stock working in the forests back then. But with time and modernization, four-wheel-drive vehicles and helicopters have slowly replaced the pack stock.

But when the Wilderness Act came into effect in 1964, it curtailed the use of motorized vehicles in the wilderness areas. Today, California has approximately 15 million acres of wilderness land that is now being threatened with wildfires year after year.[61] A vital tool in delivering supplies to firefighters in remote areas is the trusty mule, but with time, the mule has gradually been replaced with helicopters as they have become more powerful over the years. Almost twenty years ago, the USFS pack stock program was on the verge of extinction, but some dedicated Region 5 USFS mule packers campaigned and established the *Pack Stock Center of Excellence* in 2013.

This innovative program brings back some of the old-school methods of managing the forests while training packing-interns to be the next generation of packers. And in the wilderness areas, the goal is minimal impact, which can be accomplished with the use of pack mules. In present times, the mules haul in wilderness rangers and trail-crew supplies, help with certain fish-stocking projects, stock supplies for snow surveys, haul in firefighting supplies, haul in timbers for bridges, and help with other specialized projects—like hauling in 6,000 pounds of gravel to re-establish spawning beds in backcountry waters.

But why would mules be needed more than ever nowadays to help fight forest fires? As Michael Morse, the R5 Pack Stock Coordinator, explained, "Mules are an alternative tool to haul in supplies when helicopters are not available, when helicopters are not really necessary, or when the overall cost does not justify them. But there are many times when the helicopters are grounded because of darkness or thick smoke. With the recent large-scale fires in California, smoke has been a big issue hindering the use of helicopters. The packers are fire-trained, red-carded, and on-call, ready to go at a moment's notice."

On a recent fire in the Golden Trout Wilderness, a lightning strike caused a fire that became a managed wilderness fire. Morse shared, "One side of the fire was supplied by helicopters and the other side was supplied by mules. Initially, two packers and eight mules were used to assist with hauling in supplies to the fire personnel. Another string of mules was later added to help with the packing requests.

"After forty days of resupplying the fire crews, 147 mule loads were hauled to/from the fire camp, with each mule hauling an average of 175 pounds of supplies. The mules hauled a little more than 27,000 pounds of supplies averaging out to $2.81 per pound. In comparison, the helicopter hauled in approximately 99,000 pounds of supplies with an average cost of $4.91 per pound. Depending on the nature and terrain of the fire, sometimes the mules can be more advantageous than helicopters."

The USFS mules help haul in supplies for a variety of jobs— trail work, bridge and dam maintenance, fish stocking projects, and snow surveys.

These USFS mules were en route to the backcountry to bring in much-needed supplies to the fire crews. *Photo courtesy of Mike McFadin.*

120

Some may wonder—why use mules and not horses for hauling gear? The mule—a hybrid of a female horse and a male donkey—is the best animal for the job. These unsung heroes are surefooted, resilient, extremely intelligent, and very careful with their loads. Each mule can carry 150 pounds of gear and can be tied together with other mules in "mule strings." A mule string contains five mules with one packer, or ten mules with two packers, and travels about 3 mph. A string of mules can carry 1,000 to 1,500 pounds of supplies and travel twenty to thirty miles per day over treacherous trails, sometimes in darkness, and near the fireline—if safety permits it.

Loading 1,500 pounds of gear on a mule string requires a methodical approach and a special skill set that is learned over the years. It takes a lot of practice while also being a bit of an art form when balancing the loads. Lee Roeser, a second-generation packer who works for the Inyo National Forest, is regarded as one of the best packers in the Sierra Nevada. Roeser is not only very methodical in his approach to packing, but everything he does has a purpose—skills he learned over the years to ensure safety for the animal and packer.

For fire crews, Roeser shared, "We haul in food, fire tools, gasoline, medical supplies, pumps, and fire hoses. The pumps are a bit awkward and can weigh two hundred to three hundred pounds, but if broken down and loaded correctly, the mule will safely get the load delivered without any worries. In recent years, we have had to haul in communication equipment, including repeaters and two- by three-foot solar panels, which are quite fragile."

In addition to packing skills, the packer needs to have an understanding of the mules and their personalities while being passionate about their care. Ultimately, a good packer will develop trust and a good working-relationship with all his or her mules. Furthermore, packing in loads of supplies on mules is not about speed but about being prepared for any unforeseen hazards along the trail.

As part of ongoing USFS training, the packers work with fire personnel in training sessions so the firefighters can become familiar with pack stock—which is beneficial on bigger fires. Since the environment on a large fire can be a little frenzied at times, understanding how to work calmly around stock animals is in the best interest for all. Additionally, the fire crews can help be the eyes and ears for the packers on fires, keeping them informed of the fire behavior.

Another consideration on large-scale fires is all the activity around the fire camp. The fire camp can be an overwhelming and chaotic grand central station—a small city with hundreds of fire personnel scurrying around with helicopters in the background arriving and leaving on a regular basis. Pack strings have to work in unison with the helicopters delivering supplies. I wondered how the mules handle the noisy helicopters that can be working out of the same fire camp. Anyone who owns a horse or mule knows that this is not what the animal would call a "safe environment."

Roeser shared, "The art of being a good packer is knowing when and how to expose your animals to a new element and how to handle them. There have been times when I have taken a younger mule and put him or her aside and let them get used to the helicopter noise. A mule will accept the new noise sooner rather than later."

The *Pack Stock Center of Excellence* is slowly ramping up its program from its almost extinct era and still faces many challenges going forward. Today there are only ten to twelve packers among the six forests in California that manage and supply pack stock to the wilderness projects. And many of the packers wear more than one hat—some work as special-permit administrators while being on-call for packing tasks throughout the summer.

Many of these packers are reaching the top of their career, and there is no younger generation to fill their shoes. The skills they have acquired throughout their lifetimes are not easily replicated. As Lee Roeser noted, "A good packer learns his trade from the previous generation—learning all the nuances and putting in many, many miles on the trail while experiencing many different situations. Our biggest challenge presently is bringing up the next generation to take the helm and carry the program forward."

After the recent life-threatening wildfires in California, it's hard to comprehend the destruction of these fierce and powerful large-scale fires. Climate change will bring new challenges for the state and all resources need to be utilized. As a former hotshot firefighter, I am personally rooting for the USFS Pack Stock program to succeed and become a stronger resource for California's firefighting efforts.

USFS packers bring in supplies to a trail crew in the backcountry in Inyo National Forest.

Traditional packing skills are passed down from one generation to the next. Balancing a load is part "art" and part "skill." A poorly packed load can rub an animal raw or, worse, cause the mule and cargo to end up at the bottom of a canyon.

Meet and Greet: The USFS mules getting acquainted with Smokey Bear.

The *Center of Excellence* mules team up with Smokey Bear to help celebrate Smokey's seventy-fifth Birthday in 2019.

PACKER INGENUITY

The role of the USFS packer is to be knowledgeable with the stock, have extensive fire training, and be very experienced in packing for many different situations—on the trail and in a variety of fire scenarios. Ken Graves, who presently works for the Shasta-Trinity National Forest, recalls a time when he had to think outside the box to confront some fires that desperately needed attention. Multiple fires were burning throughout California in the summer of 2008, leaving no available fire crews for the smaller fires. Some small fires were burning in a wilderness area, with thick timber stands, that were threatening some nearby towns. These small fires were getting larger, and Graves felt like he had to take a stand against the fires. With only a handful of packers and some livestock, how could they build an effective fireline to help defend the towns?

"We had recently found this old trail-plow hidden in one of our facilities. It was from the 1930s, hand-forged, and specifically designed for trails. We had to re-engineer the plow so it could be pulled by a horse or a mule without a harness. So we used a good "rope horse," that was experienced with ropes, and dallied a rope from the saddle horn to pull and maneuver the plow from behind. With a few tweaks, this worked well on the trail. So we made another plow out of grader blades, welded together to make a V-shaped plow, which was also pulled by a rope horse. This plow was a bit wider than the trail plow," Graves said.

With limited equipment and manpower, this resourceful ingenuity was a saving grace for the nearby towns. They sent one guy up ahead with a chainsaw to clear trees, followed by two packers and a string of ten mules. The mules broke up the thick duff and pine needles, allowing the first trail-plow to dig a narrow trail. The wider plow followed behind, creating a wider, more effective fireline. In a two-week period, the packers, mules, and horses dug thirty miles of fireline, but it was not an easy task. Because of the daily travel to the fireline in the backcountry, they were working sixteen-hour days to get the job done. But it is these unnoticed efforts by our packers and fire crews that deserve our praise and recognition.

The packers' ingenuity helped save nearby towns by using horses and mules to dig 30 miles of fireline. *Photo Courtesy of Ken Graves.*

The USFS has utilized mule-packing since 1905, with the time-honored skills passed down from the previous generation.

A coordinated effort with biologists and packers helped relocate the rare Paiute cutthroat trout. A USFS packer was used to haul the fish cans out of the Cottonwood Creek located in a wilderness area in the White Mountains. *Photo Credit: Joe Barker.*

CHAPTER THIRTEEN

FISH STOCKING IN THE SIERRA NEVADA WITH PACK MULES

In the 1800s, Basque sheepherders were grazing in the upper Silver King Creek and noticed an unusual trout: the Paiute cutthroat trout. This rare species of fish was completely isolated and found only in this area, which today is known as the Carson-Iceberg Wilderness in the Sierra Nevada. In 1912, the Basque introduced the Paiute cutthroat trout into other headwater tributaries of the Silver King Creek watershed, which is still a very isolated area.

Since this rare species of fish is quite vulnerable to forest fire, drought, hybridization, and angling, some of the Paiute cutthroats were transplanted into Cottonwood Creek and Cabin Creek in the White Mountains Wilderness in 1946. The plan was to maintain another population source. Due to its limited habitat and enduring conservation efforts, the Paiute cutthroat has been called by local biologists "the rarest, but most recoverable fish in the United States."

In 2017, after years of devastating drought followed by flooding in California, US Fish and Wildlife Service biologists, working with members of the California Department of Fish and Wildlife (CDFW) and U.S. Forest Service (USFS), moved eighty-six "federally threatened" Paiute cutthroat trout from Cottonwood Creek (in the White Mountains) back to their native waters of Silver King Creek. This was a two-year project with the objective of enhancing the decimated populations in Silver King Creek because of the drought. Since both the Silver King Creek and Cottonwood Creek locations are in remote federal wilderness areas, pack mules were used to transport the trout.

Before the mid-1940s, the Department of Fish and Game used the old-school method of stocking trout in remote mountain lakes with pack mules and horses. The fish were transported in fish cans that look like old-fashioned milk cans, about two feet tall and eighteen inches wide, but concave on one side to fit against the pack animal. At night, the cans were set down on their sides in swift-running streams, so the water rushed in and kept the fish alive. Starting in the 1940s, airplanes were also utilized to stock high-elevation lakes in accordance with the Wilderness Act of 1964, which requires minimal actions in wilderness boundaries; this method is more economical than using pack animals. But for the fragile and limited stock of Paiute cutthroat trout, this old-school method with pack animals was utilized to have better quality control over the transport process. Luckily the Inyo National Forest has a highly qualified pack-stock program still in existence today—home of the prestigious *Pack Stock Center of Excellence.*

In the late summer of 2017, the transport project began at the North Fork of the Cottonwood Creek at an elevation just under 10,000 feet. With its cold and well-oxygenated waters, this habitat is ideal for the Paiute cutthroat trout. Biologists and pack mules made the four-mile hike in at dawn equipped with electrofishing equipment, waders, and nets. The use of electrofishing makes the job of catching fish easier for both the fish and the biologist; a small amount of electrical current passes into the water and gently stuns the fish, giving the biologist just enough time to net it. With this method, the fish are quick to recover, so the person netting has to be accurate and fast.

The captured fish spent the night in live wells in Cottonwood Creek overnight. The next day the fish were loaded onto the mules

Fish stocking was done exclusively with mules in the early 1900s. In this photo, a California Fish & Game twenty-mule pack train was carrying live California Golden Trout over Paiute Pass, elevation 11,400 feet. That summer, the snow was six feet deep on the pass. Circa: July 26, 1914. *Photo courtesy of County of Inyo, Eastern California Museum.*

in the prepared fish cans and hauled out of the White Mountains by USFS packer, Liz Vandertoorn. The fish were then transported to the Little Antelope Pack Station, near the Carson-Iceberg Wilderness, about one hundred miles northwest, in a CDFW truck outfitted with temperature controls that kept the water a constant temperature of 58°F for the long haul.

Once they reached Little Antelope Pack Station, the fish were transferred back into fish cans and loaded onto the pack mules for the final haul into Silver King Creek. Joe Cereghino, owner of the Little Antelope Pack Station, led the pack mules and two biologists, Chad Mellison and Bill Somer, into the remote part of the Carson-Iceberg Wilderness. Eight miles later, they reached the release site for the fish above Llewellyn Falls at Silver King Creek. Scientists are not known to get overly excited, but after decades of monitoring this rare species of fish, Bill Somer shared his thoughts: "Very exciting to plant fish back into Silver King Creek from North Fork Cottonwood Creek, seventy-one years later!"

This project could not have come to fruition without the old-school mule-packing methods passed down from previous generations. In today's world, scientists are armed with an arsenal of modern technology, but the use of old-fashioned fish cans and pack mules is what gets the job done. Time will tell if these conservation efforts help keep the population healthy, but for now, the eighty-six Paiute cutthroat are back home in Silver King Creek.

The fish cans are ready to be loaded on the mules at the Little Antelope Pack Station, in the Sierra Nevada.
Photo Credit: Joe Barker.

Seventy-one years later, the rare Paiute cutthroat trout were moved back to their native waters in Silver King Creek, in the Sierra Nevada. Joe Cereghino, owner of Little Antelope Pack Station, led the mules and biologists on the final leg into the Carson-Iceberg Wilderness.
Photo Credit: Joe Barker.

"Hands Across the Border," 1943, Roy Rogers, Alabama Hills, Lone Pine CA. *Photo courtesy of Museum of Western Film History, used with permission.*

CHAPTER FOURTEEN

LONE PINE AND THE MUSEUM OF WESTERN FILM HISTORY – WHERE THE WEST WAS FILMED

Driving south through the Owens Valley in the Eastern Sierra, one passes colorful cinder cones and spectacular lava flows with the large granite monuments towering above in the background. Outside of Lone Pine, the Alabama Hills emerge, offering a soft contrast to the sharp crags of the majestic Eastern Sierra. The many rounded rock features found in the Alabama Hills have been the backdrop for hundreds of Western films and television shows—including *How the West Was Won, The Ox-Bow Incident, Boots and Saddles, Gunga Din, The Nevadan, The Lone Ranger, Bonanza*, and *Rawhide*.

The breathtaking landscape has been a magnet for many directors. It is a diverse landscape that features the lowest point in the United States in the nearby stark desert of Death Valley, looming in the shadow of the highest point in the contiguous United States, Mount Whitney. It is a unique geological wonderland that could entertain a poet for hours, filling one's head with unlimited prose. Ultimately these striking and raw landscapes helped create and inspire the dramatic narrative of the iconic Western.

For one hundred years, the Lone Pine area has been a favorite Western film location, hosting many cattle drives, gunfights, wagon trains, and Indian battles. And filming continues there today with scenes in *Iron Man, Star Trek VII*, and *Django Unchained* utilizing this famous backdrop. Additionally, many commercials are filmed in the hills, keeping the rosters filled throughout the year.

The Alabama Hills have been graced with many larger-than-life actors—John Wayne, Gene Autry, Randolph Scott, Clint Eastwood, Gregory Peck, and William Boyd, who portrayed Hopalong Cassidy. The cowboys of the silver screen have been our role models of the Old West. These memorable cowboys rode their horses, shot their guns, entertained us with their songs, and provided law and order. We have a special place in our hearts for them, and they will always be our heroes. Additionally, they left their mark on a generation of children in the mid-1900s: Kids loved to imitate the Lone Ranger, galloping around in their living rooms with animated shouts of "Hi-Yo-Silver."

If you are a Western film buff, no trip is complete to the Sierra without a visit to the Museum of Western Film History, located in Lone Pine. The museum takes pride in noting that they are "surrounded by the largest Western back-lot in the country." Quietly stepping back in time, the museum pays tribute to the first film shot in the Alabama Hills in 1920—*The Round Up*, a silent Western starring Roscoe "Fatty" Arbuckle as Sheriff Slim Hoover. The museum also has forty ongoing and top-notch exhibits with plenty of memorabilia and behind-the-scenes photos from iconic films to inspire you. Throughout the museum, you will find some fantastic movie props: the dentist's wagon from *Django Unchained*, the Overland Stagecoach from *Rawhide*, the car Humphrey Bogart drove in *High Sierra*, a variety of period-piece costumes, and a few rifles and muskets from different films. Going to the museum is a great way to become acquainted with the early Western films. I guarantee that after a visit, you will be filled with nostalgia and want to add a few of these old, classic movies to your Netflix queue.

While visiting the Alabama Hills, it is worth watching the sunrise along "Movie Road"—an experience that is beyond words. Exploring the different canyons and landmarks takes you back to an era from long ago. This area is just as it was one hundred years ago—unchanged and unspoiled, since the land is managed by the Bureau of Land Management. Pick up a copy of Dave Holland's

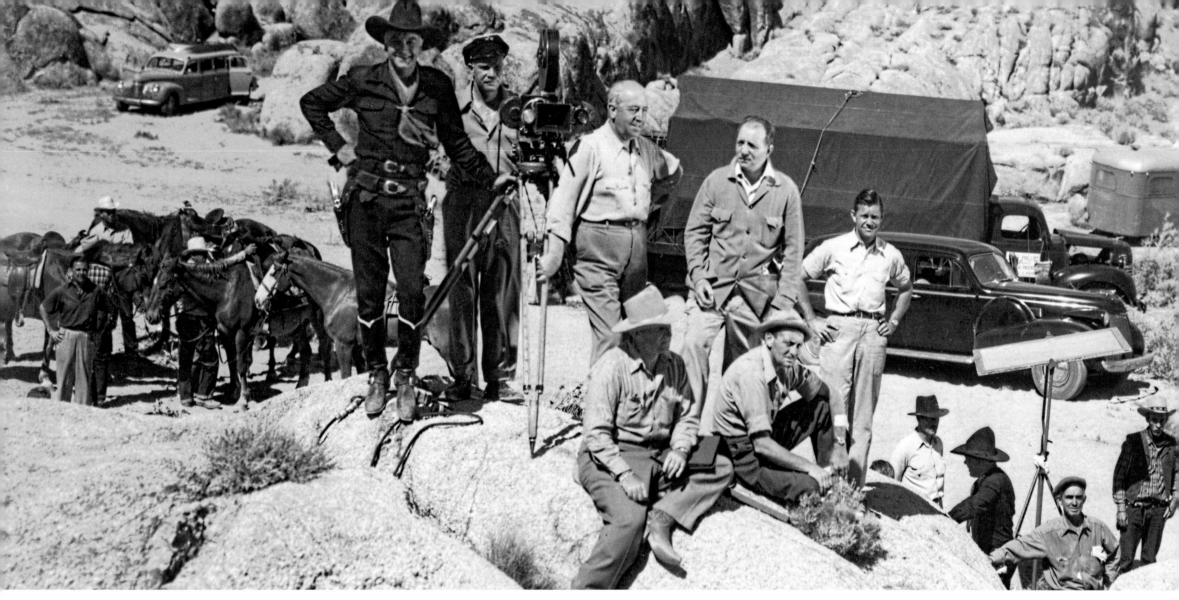

Hopalong Cassidy (William Boyd), Alabama Hills, Lone Pine, CA. *Photo courtesy of Museum of Western Film History, used with permission.*

book, *On Location in Lone Pine,* or the self-guided map from the museum; they will guide you to the various landmarks and provide an insight into the storied past of the Alabama Hills. There is never a shortage of behind-the-scenes stories.

If you can't get enough fill of your Western film nostalgia, then it might be worth signing up for some of the events at the Lone Pine Film Festival, held annually over the Columbus Day weekend in October. The festival includes a gala reception, film screenings, movie location tours, celebrity guest speakers, Wild West shows,

and some cowboy poetry. Without a doubt, the festival makes for a fun-filled weekend.

The Alabama Hills is truly a magical place where Western movies come alive!

I recall Robert Duvall telling me, "The English have Shakespeare; the French have Molière; we, as Americans, have Westerns."

—*Hostiles* writer-director Scott Cooper.

Alabama Hills

Saddle up for a dramatic rendezvous with memories,
Of how the Wild West was won and lost, and where
The new era of motion pictures was prominently filmed,
The "Hills" provide a natural backdrop beyond compare.

Deep shadows accentuate the monument contours,
Supernatural rock formations change with the moving light.
Ancient sculptures carved by wind, water, and time,
Dance with their bedfellows laced with quartzite.

Entangled in huge sandstone boulders and sagebrush,
The Hills have hosted numerous film locations of long ago:
From Nevada and California, Utah, to Texas and Arizona,
South to Peru and Argentina and even down to Old Mexico.

Saved from the jaws of notoriety by motion picture film,
Old Westerns come a rip-roaring through the rocks and rills.
Come a ridin' all those resilient riders of yesteryear,
Masquerading 'neath costumes, stunts, scripts, and thrills.

Ghost riders of Dukes', Mixes', Rogers', and Rangers',
Were rescued from obscurity by the science of light,
Cowboys and Indians alike left their marks in time,
Captured from extinction in color, and black and white.

Introducing silhouettes from canyons' shadowy curtains,
A sharp sliver of sunlight pierces a spotlight on stage.
Whirling of stagecoach wheels and pounding of hooves
Break the silence with the wind of another age.

In the midst of a dwindling campfire's flickering light,
Twilight only pales the remnants of history's past…
An era of outlaws, renegades, heroes, and heroines,
All preserved in motion pictures, immortalizing the cast.

© Sallie Knowles Joseph

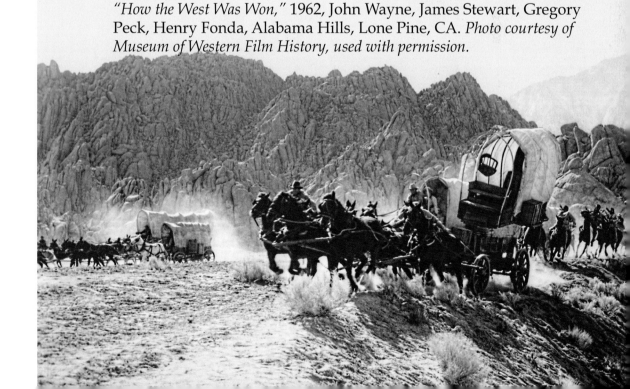

"Under Western Stars," 1938, Roy Rogers, Alabama Hills, Lone Pine, CA. *Photo courtesy of Museum of Western Film History, used with permission.*

"How the West Was Won," 1962, John Wayne, James Stewart, Gregory Peck, Henry Fonda, Alabama Hills, Lone Pine, CA. *Photo courtesy of Museum of Western Film History, used with permission.*

CHAPTER FIFTEEN

RANCH RODEO IN THE SIERRA NEVADA

With much anticipation, the crowd patiently waits for the next bronc rider to take center stage, as the bronc horse fiercely snorts and clanks around in the chute. With much respect, the cowboy calmly mounts the horse, getting his gear in order. Taking a deep breath, he signals to the gatekeeper that he is ready and the chute opens. As the drama unfolds, the horse gets some height before it bucks with extraordinary grace and strength. During those long eight seconds, the suspenseful climax approaches—with either the rider surviving the ordeal or getting bucked off the beast.

For many of the spectators, the bronc riding competition is perhaps the most exhilarating event of the rodeo performances. Contrary to the myths about the "broncs," these modern bronc horses are bred specifically as bucking stock; they are not wild horses that cowboys, from past generations, had to mount.

Before I mount, my heart's just pounding. When I mount the horse, everything starts to go blank. When the chute opens, I try to keep my mind in the middle and HOLD ON TIGHT. It's a rough ride…and you hope for the best.

—*Matt Johnston, 2016 Bridgeport Ranch Rodeo Bronc Riding Winner.*

Modern rodeo competitions can be traced back to cattle herding practices that expanded into the West from the early Spanish and Mexican vaqueros. The supreme roping skills and horsemanship of the vaqueros were passed along to the American cowboy in the mid-1800s. In the late 1800s, Wild West Shows traveled throughout the country, where the charismatic Buffalo Bill Cody entertained the crowds with his bulldogging tricks. Present-day rodeos became an offshoot of these traveling shows. Today there are many local rodeos in addition to the professional rodeo circuit throughout the state of California.

But a more traditional type of rodeo—the "ranch rodeo"—evolved from competitions between working-ranches. Instead of watching professionally-trained rodeo cowboys compete, the ranch rodeo is the real deal—with ranch-hands taking a break from cattle chores to compete in this social and competitive event. Each ranch competes as a team in the competitions, with a top-prize awarded to the best ranch or team. Additionally, there are a few individual awards in today's ranch rodeos.

With the stunning Eastern Sierra as a backdrop, the annual Bridgeport Ranch Rodeo is held every Fourth of July at the Centennial Livestock Arena, in Bridgeport, California. The rodeo is organized by the Bridgeport Gun Club and there is never a shortage of community charm and spirit in this mountain ranching town. The rodeo includes team roping, bronc riding, steer stopping, double mugging, team doctoring, trailer loading, branding, and a women's division. Additionally, the Fourth of July celebration also includes a parade, BBQ, and fireworks.

Throughout the Sierra Nevada, there are many rodeo events with top-caliber performances. Many of these rodeos and ranch rodeos are part of western festivals that celebrate the early pioneers and cowboys that helped settle the state in the 1800s.

"Courage is being scared to death, but saddling up anyway."

—John Wayne

Left: Airborne – Holdin' on Tight!

Below: Perfectly framed loop.

The women's division
has plenty of talented
cowgirls.

Startin' young and
dreamin' big.

The Calling

When the chute opens, leather fringe explodes
And spur tips ignite the bronc-riders dance.
Like the grace of an airborne manta ray,
Both united by the temptress of chance.

The cheers from the crowd go completely unnoticed,
Drowned by two heartbeats, with respect – not fear.
Both beings on a "high" of complex adrenaline,
Marching to a drumbeat only they can hear.

A thousand pounds of raw un-bridled energy,
As hooves strike the ground with unmeasured force.
If not calculated correctly, the opposing force can be flight
And a rhythm is established between man and horse.

Eight seconds can seem like an eternity,
Yet to some, there's never a time to be done.
Parting company is bittersweet but inevitable,
Leaving a score in the combined shadow of one.

© Sallie Knowles Joseph

"Courage is resistance to fear, mastery of fear, not absence of fear."

—Mark Twain

The women's winning team, Diamond Y Bar, showing how it's done in the team roping event.

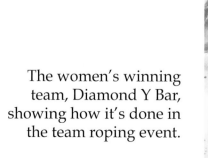

The Eastern Sierra provides a stunning backdrop for the Bridgeport Ranch Rodeo.

No shortage of great views at the Bridgeport Ranch Rodeo.

A packer coming into the finish line with his string of mules in the Individual Packer Scramble.

CHAPTER SIXTEEN

BISHOP MULE DAYS: THE GREATEST MULE SHOW ON EARTH

The year was 1969. The Eastern Sierra was recovering from a record snowfall, trying to dig its way out in the springtime. Bishop tourism was taking a big hit. The pack stations were sitting idle with the packers wondering when the snow would melt so they could welcome visitors into the High Sierra. Leo Porterfield, the trails and maintenance supervisor for Inyo National Forest, proposed an idea of hosting an event that might help tourism in the spring—an event that would highlight the mules, the U.S. Forest Service, and the history of the Eastern Sierra. Porterfield discussed it with Wilfred Partridge and Bob Tanner. However, the packers were skeptical—"Who would be interested in watching what we do?"

A committee was formed and, with careful planning, the first "Mule Day" event was launched over Memorial Day weekend in 1970. This one-day show and parade was a huge success and the rest is history.

Fifty years later, Bishop Mule Days is a six-day celebration showcasing five hundred amazing mules and donkeys in a variety of competitions, including Western, English, sprint races, cattle work, trail trials, team roping, chariot racing, gymkhana, coon jumping, and a variety of driving competitions. Bishop Mule Days is a celebration like none other…in the world, for that matter. It is one part mule show, one part rodeo, and the other part is an unpredictable Wild West show. The mule, the unsung hero in the equine world, is the main attraction of the week-long celebration attracting more than 30,000 visitors from all over the world.

At Bishop Mule Days, you'll see some of the most stunning mules and donkeys. "That can't be a donkey," you'll hear visitors say while

A close finish in the four-hundred-yard sprint race.

The finishes for the Packer Scramble events can be spectacular, with team members frantically making sure everything is tied down correctly while sprinting to the finish line.

A restored 1902 steam fire engine, built by American LaFrance for the city of Reno. It makes an appearance at Bishop Mule Days, pulled by three draft mules.

Leaning into the turn, Gyp and
Jude win the Chariot Barrel Race,
setting a new world record.

The stunning Sierra Nevada is
the backdrop for Bishop
Mule Days.

watching in disbelief. You will see mules and donkeys performing in obstacle courses, jumps, and even a sprint finish. The college teams provide some great entertainment and creativity showing off their mules in a costume contest—Ninja Turtle mules, the musical group "Kiss," and pirate mules come to mind.

There is no shortage of entertainment, but the crowd favorites among all the events are the various packer-scramble competitions. In the scrambles, the mules and horses are released in the arena, a blank gunshot goes off to stampede the herd, and all the animals scatter in different directions—running back and forth like a game of tag while dodging the gear, judges, and packers. There is always that one special mule that proudly runs circles around the arena with a lone packer helplessly trying to catch him. The teams must collect all their mules and horses, pack them correctly, and then ride them around the quarter-mile track. The finishes can be spectacular, with the team members frantically making sure everything is tied down correctly while sprinting to the finish line.

Trent Peterson, lead packer of the Rock Creek Pack Station team, shares his thoughts about competing in the scramble: "It's pure chaos…we have ourselves running into a stampeding herd, which you wouldn't normally do in any circumstance. The whole concept of a packer scramble is pure insanity, and the crowd loves it!"

After the initial success of Bishop Mule Days, other mule events popped up around the country. But Bishop remains the big-daddy of the mule shows, with riders competing for bragging rights and World Championship titles. Obtaining the *High Point Mule* award is one of the highest achievements at Bishop Mule Days, but it takes a very special mule to get all those points. *High Point* involves placing in the top-ten in a lot of events to generate points. Bryce Hathaway started competing with his beloved pack-mule, White Trash, at Mule Days in 2004. But he soon realized that he would have to step up his game if he ever wanted to win the *High Point* award—an award that requires superior versatility.

Hathaway shares, "To win the award, I had to train my mule to transition from being a really good pack-mule to being a really good show mule—teaching her that when we changed the saddle and bit for English riding, she needed to keep her head up high and stride out more. And ten minutes later, she had to adapt and change her gait when we put on the western saddle for the next event. Additionally, she had to be good at driving to get a lot of points. As a comparison, in the horse world, a horse only competes in one specialty—English, Western, or driving, not all three."

In 2017, Hathaway and White Trash proudly won the *High Point* award, elating many fans. Hathaway might be a serious competitor in some events, but his sense of humor and derelict maneuvers regularly entertain the crowds in the non-competitive events—like the Dolly Parton Contest and Musical Tires—earning White Trash her own fan club in the stands.

Compared to horse shows, there is a different energy at Bishop Mule Days. Owning and training a mule can be a humbling experience. Mules are smart, and it's best not to get an inflated head around one, or they will remind you otherwise. Additionally, at Mule Days, the competitors share much more camaraderie among one another. They may be serious in competition but will walk away as friends after the event, supporting one another. And everyone is there to have a good time. There is never a dull moment to be had with so many entertaining events—events that you will not find at any other venue.

With the Eastern Sierra as a backdrop, the streets of Bishop come alive Saturday morning as the rural town hosts one of the largest non-motorized parades with more than a hundred entertaining entries. The Bishop Mule Day's parade varies from year to year, but the entries are unique to the area. It is common to see decorated mules, plenty of pack strings, hitch wagons, wagon trains, BLM donkeys, and Wild West themed entries. But the visitors patiently wait to see their two favorite entries—the *Range of Light Mule String* and the twenty mule team. Lee and Jen Roeser lead the *Range of Light Mule String* with the mules proudly displaying the American flags in honor of the Memorial Day holiday. Their twenty mules can be seen maneuvering down Main Street, each displaying flowers in remembrance, with flags gently blowing in the breeze.

And off in the distance, the rhythmic sound of bells and chains can be heard getting closer and closer. People crowd the streets, trying to catch a glimpse of the twenty mule team pulling the 8000-pound borax wagons. These replica wagons and the mule team made

There are many exciting finishes at the Packer Scramble events.

Left: The *Range of Light Mule String* celebrates the Memorial Day holiday with their American flag presentation.

Below: A mule demonstrates great jumping ability in the Hunter Class.

Opposite, top left: Bob Tanner was one of the key founders of Bishop Mule Days. In this photo, Tanner's grandson proudly leads a string of mules through the streets of Bishop in the parade.

Opposite, top right: Donkeys can be trained to jump and participate in a variety of Gymkhana events. This stunning donkey is demonstrating his abilities in the Pole Bending event.

Opposite, bottom left: An eight-mule hitch entertains the crowds at the 50th Anniversary.

Opposite, bottom right: Mules do exceptionally well in the team roping and steer stopping events.

The *Range of Light Mule String* getting ready for the parade.

Opposite, top left: Working on a fast finish for the Pole Bending event.

Opposite, top right: *The Start of the Team Packer Scramble* – the packers must collect their mules and horses, pack them correctly, and then ride them around the quarter-mile track.

Opposite, bottom left: White Trash, the *High Point Mule* in 2017, entertains the crowds in a variety of events.

Opposite, bottom right: Mules can pack a variety of odd items, such as coolers, chairs, and large cookstoves.

their inaugural appearance at Bishop Mule Days in 1981 (see the chapter on the Twenty Mule Team). Since 1981, Bobby Tanner has guided the team through the streets of Bishop and into the arena for a second performance—demonstrating to the crowds the "jumping of the chain" for a close-up view. The "jumping of the chain" is a technique used only on long-line hitches, allowing the team to make a turn.

For any newcomer, Mule Days will put to rest any misconceptions you have about a mule. I regularly hear, "I didn't know that mules can jump." These lovable creatures with their adorable long-ears will win over even the staunchest horse-enthusiast. Walking around the fairgrounds, you'll hear the occasional "bray" or "aw-ah-aw," making the kids squeal with delight. The mules and donkeys are just sending out a friendly reminder that they are the kings of the show.

The best way to fully appreciate Mule Days is to come for the week—not just for the day. If you bring your RV and camp in the fairgrounds, you will take home a few extra stories and make several new friends—guaranteed! Another way to get involved with Mule Days is to volunteer. I have suggested it to a number of friends, and they always report how much fun they have riding security patrol on their horse or mule—meeting hundreds of folks along the way. The six-day celebration is filled with BBQ dinners, concerts, dances, western exhibits, cowboy church, and breakfasts. And if you see me floating around the arena with three cameras in tow, please be sure to say "hi!"

The new replica wagons, built by Dave Engel and owned by the Death Valley Conservancy, made their first appearance in Death Valley National Park, in November of 2019.

CHAPTER SEVENTEEN

TWENTY MULE TEAM

One of the great icons of the Old West was the Borax 20 Mule Teams® of Death Valley. Few corporate jingles or logos capture the dust, grit, and western spirit of California's rich history like the Borax 20 Mule Team®. From 1884 through 1888, the twenty mule teams delivered their twenty-ton borax loads to and from Death Valley and Mojave with timetable precision. This astounding mule transport was later celebrated in the successful radio and television series, "Death Valley Days," where it became a household name in the advertising campaign promoting 20 Mule Team Borax Soap.

Today we still celebrate these amazing mule accomplishments with the twenty mule team making annual appearances at Bishop Mule Days, the Big Hitch Parade in Idaho (where they pull six antique ore-wagons), along with special appearances at the Tournament of Roses Parade, Death Valley, Boron, California, and Washington, D.C.

In 1881 Aaron Winters discovered a major borax deposit near what is now the Furnace Creek Ranch. Within a few years, William T. Coleman bought up most of the borax claims in Death Valley and built the Harmony Borax Works. But to make the mining operation possible, he had to haul the borax to the nearest railroad line in Mojave—a 165-mile trip one way.

In the 1800s, large mule teams were in common use throughout the western states, hauling freight to and from railroad lines. Mules

One of the great icons of the Old West was the Borax 20 Mule Teams of Death Valley. In this photo, a twenty mule team was re-enacting the trip from Mojave to Death Valley in 1936. *Photo courtesy of County of Inyo, Eastern California Museum.*

Starting from a dead-stop, the twenty mule team is getting into cadence. Visually, the photo is a "sea of ears" coming out of the dust.

The impressive seven-foot-diameter wheels are prominent in this photo, offering a size comparison to the mules.

were chosen for this demanding job because they were well-suited for the task of pulling these huge wagons in the desert—mules tolerate heat better, require less water, and have superior stamina. The twenty mule teams in Death Valley were unique because of the enormous payloads they hauled across the hottest, driest, lowest desert in the West.

To make the borax mining venture more profitable, Coleman commissioned J.W.S. Perry to build wagons large enough to haul at least ten tons in each wagon (twenty tons for two wagons). But such wagons did not exist! Big freight wagons had been used extensively since the 1850s, but up to that time, the largest payload that could be hauled by a two-wagon train was fifteen tons. So, Perry went to Mojave to seek out the expertise needed to help build ten of these great wagons—for the new desert "freight train."

The grueling 330-mile, twenty-day roundtrip journey through the mostly roadless and desolate desert required a superior wagon that would hold up to the demanding task at hand. And what an amazing wagon Perry designed: seven-foot-diameter rear wheels that were eight inches wide, eighteen-inch-diameter hubs, and sixteen-foot-long beds constructed of solid oak. Each wagon weighed 7,800 pounds, costing about $900 each.[62] All ten wagons (five teams) were in constant use from 1884 through 1888 without a single break-down—achieving their lofty goals. Some joked that they were built so well that "they'll roll forever." In 1890, Coleman's borax holdings were acquired by Francis Marion Smith, who then formed the Pacific Coast Borax Company.

In the five years of operation, the mule teams hauled over 20 million pounds of borax out of Death Valley.[63] This massive movement of borax could not have been accomplished without the impressive mule teams and the mighty teamster. Only two men worked the team—a teamster and a swamper, who assisted with the chores and operated the brake in the rear wagon. The teamster was also affectionately referred to as a "muleskinner" in that era.

Muleskinner: A professional mule driver or teamster who drives mules.

The term "skinner" is slang for someone who might "skin" or outsmart a mule, since mules are known for their intelligence and situational caution. Also, there were times when the muleskinner rode on one of the animals and used a "jerk line" to control and steer the leaders. The term, muleskinner, was first used by John Beadle in his 1870 book, *Life in Utah*. In modern times, the term is not used much except to denote those who drove the big mule teams.

Life on the Death Valley desert was filled with many hardships and was extremely dangerous for the teamsters. John R. Spears, a reporter for the *New York Sun*, traveled hundreds of miles in the desert interviewing the borax kings, miners, and teamsters. Spears noted, "There are grades like the one on the road from Granite Spring to Mojave, where the plunge is steep. The load must go down, so when the brink is reached, the driver throws his weight on the brake of the front wagon, the swamper handles the brake on the rear, and away they go—creaking, groaning, and sliding until the bottom is reached.

"If the brake holds, all is well, but now and then a brake-block gives way, then a race with death begins. With yells and curses, the long team is started in a gallop—an effort is made to swing around up the mountainside, a curve is reached, and if an animal falls, or a wheel strikes a rock or a rut, and, with a thunderous crash, over go the great wagons. There are many graves on the desert of men who have died with their boots on, but some of them hold-men were killed striving to guide a runaway freight team in a wild dash down the side of a desert mountain."[64]

On a more humorous note, to get the mule team to pull a thirty-five-ton "overall weight" load from a standstill, the teamster had his own set of commands for the team, usually flowered with a few expletives—"Git up, you __ __ – git up!" Spears shared one story, "It is a matter of record that the mules understood him… and only once failed to understand the driver. On that occasion, he had gone to hear the evangelist preach, and had been converted. Next morning, it is said, when he mounted the wagon and invited the team to go on—the mules, with one accord, turned their heads over their shoulders, cocked forward their ears and stared at him. He had omitted the customary expletive from his command."[65]

People crowd the streets trying to catch a glimpse of the twenty mule team pulling the 8000-pound borax wagons at the Bishop Mule Days parade.

PRESENT-DAY TWENTY MULE EXHIBITION TEAM

In 1981, Bobby Tanner, his father Bob Tanner, George Chamberlain, and Leaky Olivas got together and dreamed up the idea of bringing back the twenty mule team to exhibit at the next Bishop Mule Days. Combining their mules—ten from the Tanners and ten from Chamberlain—they came up with a big team. Additionally, they partnered with US Borax Company to use one of the remaining sets of promotional borax wagons to complete the team.

At the time, Bobby Tanner had never driven a big team. But Olivas had worked with the previous twenty mule team, doing demonstrations in the 1950s in Lone Pine. Olivas was familiar with how that hitch was set up and passed on his knowledge to the next generation. Bobby Tanner noted, "It took a lot of time and practice to learn all the intricacies and details of operating a twenty mule team—the hitch is very different from modern-day hitches."

He added, "The hitch was designed for function. It was a very efficient hitch designed to deliver the most power in the desert terrain while being the easiest on the animals. Because of this specialized hitch, the team could be controlled with only a 'jerk line' (a single rein) and the weight of the wagon. These were real working

Top: *The First Hitch* – the twenty mule team pulling the new replica wagons for the first time in 2016 in preparation for the Rose Parade. *Photo Credit: Merilee Mitchell.*

Bottom: Bobby Tanner helped spearhead the campaign to bring back the twenty mule team to exhibit at Bishop Mule Days.

Driving the long-line team

Mules were hitched in pairs to a chain that stretched 100 feet in front of the wagons. Each pair had a special job — Leaders steered the teams, Pointers jumped the chain to guide the wagons around sharp turns, and the Wheelers and Swing teams provided traction and power.

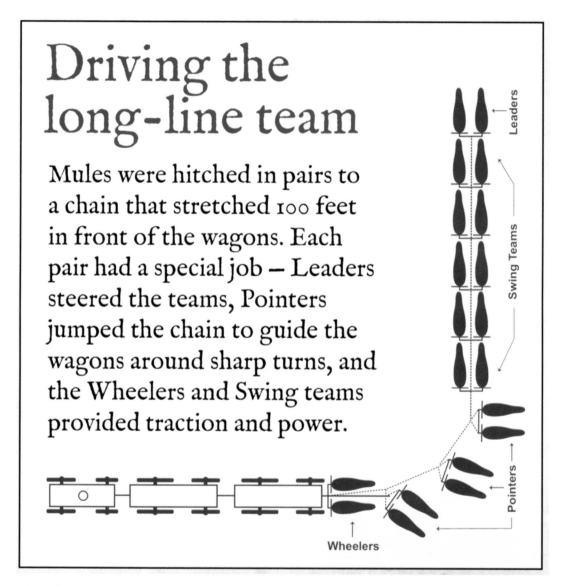

This drawing demonstrates how the pointers jump the chain.

mules, unlike the fancy hitches seen nowadays that pull minimal loads and are controlled with driving reins."

So they went out and practiced on a wide, open road outside of Bishop, learning all the nuances of driving the big team. The twenty mule team is made up of two lead mules called the "leaders" with the left-handed "near" mule controlled by a single jerk line, which in turn controls the whole team. The next five pairs are called "swing teams," whose main job is to stop, start, and provide a lot of power. The next three pairs are the "pointers," which have a very important role. These mules are specially trained "to jump over the one-hundred-foot chain," which is connected to all the mules lengthwise. When making a turn, the mules jump the chain, while moving to the side, pulling away from the curve to keep the chain tight—up to a 45-degree angle. The last pair is the "wheelers." The role of the wheelers has been misidentified over the years "as being draft horses that provide the power to the team."

Bobby Tanner noted, "The role of the wheelers has often been mischaracterized—the true role of the horses was to provide a 'bell mare' for the mules. At night there were miles of empty desert for the mules to run, but by nature, mules like to follow a horse. So if you tied up the horses, particularly a mare, the mules would not wander and the teamster would have his mules close by in the morning.

"Also the wheeler position was a place to hide weaker animals. Horses, especially the 'cold blood' draft horses (generally from colder regions in the world), do not do well in the harsh desert climate. And the wheelers have little to do with the steering of the wagon—another mischaracterization. The single trees and spreader of the pointers are attached to the front-end of the tongue. Thus, the pointers are responsible for the steering of the wagon."

Tanner also noted that the wheeler horses needed to be strong enough to accommodate a rider. In rough terrain with numerous uphills and curves, the teamster might choose to ride the "near" wheeler (left side)—this position enabled the teamster to encourage the wheelers and pointers to work a little harder.

With lots of practice in 1981, 21-year-old Bobby Tanner became a master of the jerk line and "jumping the chain." Their debut at Bishop Mule Days was a smashing success and celebrated the role of the working mule—a tradition that has been carried

The Dancing Mules, a painting by Dan Taylor, depicts the pointers jumping the chain on the turn. *Photo courtesy of US Borax.*

forward to present-day. Not to be missed, the most exciting part of watching the twenty mule team is witnessing them make a turn while "jumping the chain."

And another alluring feature of the twenty mule team is the bells worn by the leader mules. They provide an unforgettable, harmonious sound that captivates the crowds today. In the desert, the leaders wore bells to warn oncoming traffic, but the teamsters also believed the bells helped "strike a rhythm" that kept the mules in a groove that caused them to walk a half-mile an hour farther.

Today the twenty mule team makes a few special appearances throughout the year. But in the summer, you'll find these endearing mules in the glorious backcountry of the Sierra Nevada, packing for Red's Meadow Pack Station—owned by Bobby and Claudia Tanner.

RECREATING HISTORY

Today, the only remaining set of original, 1880s wagons can be seen at Harmony Borax Works in Death Valley. They are no longer road-worthy. Over the years, the twenty mule team used the US Borax Company's promotional wagon-sets for exhibitions. But the promotional wagons had a lot of years on them. So twenty years

The newly constructed water wagon can be seen in this photo, making its debut at the 50th Anniversary of Bishop Mule Days.

ago, there was a campaign to keep the legend alive and recreate a new set of full-sized wagons for the exhibiting team. Bobby Tanner, the US Borax company leaders, and the Death Valley Conservancy worked in tandem to make this vision come alive.

In 2016, the Death Valley Conservancy raised funds and commissioned Dave Engel—of Engel's Coach Shop in Montana—to build the replica wagons. Engel used measurements from the Harmony wagons and historical photos to recreate precise, full-size copies of the original wagons. These magnificent, new freight wagons made their glorious debut at the 2017 Rose Parade in Pasadena,

California. Continuing this vision, Engel also built a water wagon that made its debut at the 50th Anniversary of Bishop Mule Days in 2019. When not in use, the replica wagons are on display at Law's Museum outside of Bishop, California.

"I had to look at the original wagons through the eyes of a nine-teenth-century wagon maker and understand how they thought—we were doing a re-creation of the wagons, not an imitation."

—Dave Engel, Engel's Coach Shop, Joliet, Montana.

In 2017, the Big Hitch assembled twenty-one mules and horses pulling a sixteen-foot disc.

CHAPTER EIGHTEEN

THE BIG HITCH

There is a dedicated group of teamsters that gets together every few years in Sierraville (in the Sierra Nevada) or parts of the Central Valley. These teamsters have one common goal—keeping the tradition of pulling old farm equipment with equine power alive and passing along this valuable information to the next generation. In a world of technological advances and abundant gadgets, these old traditions are becoming a lost art among the present generation.

I was invited to follow this event for four days in late June of 2017, which was organized by Luke Messenger, who has been driving for more than twenty years. I met Messenger and some of the other teamsters at various events and heard all the talk about their Big Hitch event. I was thrilled to attend and watch the process of working a big hitch—a multi-day process.

I first wondered how this particular hitch started. According to Messenger, "I started working with George Cabral in 2008, who was asked by the Antique Caterpillar Machine Owners Club (ACMOC) to put together a mule team to pull a 1904 Holt, a ground-driven hill-side combine." *Ground driven* refers to the power being provided by the draft of the animals—no engine power. The group was led by George Cabral, who provided the expertise in hooking the mules; Gene Hilti, an expert in the art of big hitches; and Paul Reno, who collected and restored the Schandoney Hitch. The group of teamsters successfully hooked twenty-seven mules to pull the combine that year.

Messenger adds, "There were many helpers that year, and I was one of them…and I always found myself under a mule. There were many owners who helped and contributed to the effort—no one owner supplied more than four mules. And most of the mules had never worked together before, making it a meaningful experience."

In 2011, Messenger was asked by event organizers to put together thirty-two mules to pull the same combine, as part of the ACMOC show called *Best Show on Tracks*. *Best Show on Tracks* is an event commemorating the founding of the Caterpillar Tractor Company in 1925 by the merger of the Holt and Best tractor companies—resulting in the largest gathering of antique Best, Caterpillar, and Holt tractors.

Messenger agreed to organize the hitch only if Cabral and Hilti assisted in the effort. That year they successfully hooked up thirty-three mules with Messenger, Cabral, and Hilti taking turns driving the mules—a memory cherished for all involved. The partnership with Cabral passed along a wealth of knowledge to all involved in those hitches. The beloved Cabral passed away in 2014, and fortunately, some of his expertise has been passed down to the next generation of teamsters trying to keep the tradition alive.

In recent years, Messenger has assembled three hitches: 2012 Sierraville Hitch, 2014 Hennigan Farms Hitch, and the hitch I attended—the 2017 Stoney Creek Shire Ranch Hitch. The 2017 Hitch was targeting a hitch of thirty-three horses and mules pulling a sixteen-foot disc, but the heat became an obstacle to achieving that goal. The teamsters and animals had to endure the blistering heat of 110°F through most of the week. Because of the forecasted heat, there were many cancellations. It was a bit disappointing for those who organized the event, but there was a lot of knowledge

Molly and Kate: Percheron mules that Luke Messenger acquired from his mentor, George Cabral.

This modern photo of working mules is reminiscent of the draft animals on the farm a century ago.

and expertise still to be shared among the group. The hitch ultimately succeeded in hitching twenty-one animals: seventeen mules and four horses.

Many of us are acquainted with the big hitches used to haul freight—like the Borax twenty mule teams and the Big Hitch in Alberta, Canada. In the late 1800s, many of the working freight hitches used ten-ups and twelve-ups (horses or mules paired in tandem). To pull the farm equipment, the Schandoney Hitch was utilized because it was designed to equalize the loads among spans of six abreast. Additionally, the six abreast spans allowed more horses or mules to be used in close proximity to the driver, allowing for better control and turning capability in the field.

As Messenger notes, "The challenge with hooking up the Schandoney Hitch is timing and tuning all the animals to work as

Taking a break while adjustments are made to the hitch.

one unit. Once all the adjustments have been made, the hook-up is relatively quick, and the operation is very smooth."

He also added, "When we first start to assemble these hitches, we usually have some animals that have not worked together and many of them have never worked six abreast. We are very mindful of safety for both man and beast. With that said, we begin by working with individual groups of six abreast with the leaders in the front. We always use a safety measure to stop the team if needed. This year

we used a sixteen-foot hydraulic disc. Other times, we have simply pulled a heavy truck."

As the spans of six are worked and tweaked, the teamsters get a better idea of what order each span will have in the hitch. Usually, the better-behaved and mature animals will be near the front. Once the spans are "trained to drive six abreast," the teamsters hook all the spans together. Initially, the teamsters have lines on every span and enough drivers on the cart to handle the lines.

Luke Messenger also pulls old farm equipment with his four Percherons in an effort to keep horse-powered farming techniques alive in this century. Pulling plows, scrapers, and harrows is a time-honored tradition that died off by the mid-1900s.

As time progresses and adjustments are made, Messenger begins to take lines off one span at a time. Proudly Messenger states, "By Saturday, we were driving only the leaders. We had lines on the wheel span as a safety precaution, but they were held slack."

Asked how he deals with challenging animals, Messenger shared, "We usually have at least one or two mules that have very limited or sometimes no experience in a bigger hitch. I always find this challenge to be the most rewarding and it's an excellent time to introduce an animal to this type of work. If they are tied in correctly, they can throw their fits and it only affects them. It is wonderful to see how quickly they figure it out."

From my perspective, this was living history at its best. I was never prouder to be a part of this group while watching their efforts evolve over a four-day period. It will be interesting to follow this group over the next decade or two. As Rick Edney sums it up, "I have been involved with four big hitches with my first one mentored by Cabral and Hilti. They possessed a huge wealth of knowledge and always had an answer to any questions that arose. They are both gone now along with our safety net, so it is up to us to keep educating ourselves and keep the big hitch going."

The Wareing Shires — from Blackfoot, Idaho — coming into the lineup.

CHAPTER NINETEEN
DRAFT HORSE CLASSIC

When the arena fills up with six-horse hitches of Percherons, Belgians, Shires, and Clydesdales, there is no room for error as the teams trot around the show ring entertaining the crowds. There is nothing more exhilarating than feeling the ground move as one of these six-ton teams parades past you with amazing grace and their heads held high. And when it comes to draft horse hitches, the fans always line up to see the six-horse hitches because, in their mind, "the more, the better."

Now in its thirty-fourth year, the annual Draft Horse Classic of Nevada County is a premier draft horse show on the West Coast offering six different performances over four days in September. The Draft Horse Classic is unique in that it combines many different elements, including a farm class, the Americana class, a farm implement class, youth classes, pleasure competitions, hitch competitions, an obstacle competition, and log skidding. There are also many entertainment acts, including the mule chuck wagon races, the Bobby Kerr Mustang Act, the California Cowgirls Drill Team, and the CHP Mounted Patrol Unit. Additionally, the Harvest Fair is simultaneously happening on the fairgrounds—featuring horseshoe demonstrations, musical entertainment, art exhibits, and plenty of delicious food.

With almost two hundred horses competing, the competitors come from across the United States and Canada. These horses are stabled on the grounds of the Nevada County Fairgrounds in Grass Valley, offering spectators the unique opportunity to meet and marvel at these gentle giants up close—when the barns are open to the public. With a variety of horses and hitches, there is no shortage of entertainment throughout the weekend.

Our nation was built with the help of draft horses—from hauling loads to distant towns, providing the horsepower to cultivate the soil in farm fields, in scraping and leveling roadways, extracting logs from forests, and helping to move freight throughout the West during the nineteenth century. The farmer and his team of horses had to learn to work skillfully as a team to get the job done. Similarly, the much-admired horse hitches at the Draft Horse Classic are trained throughout the year, learning to work well as a team. As one teamster shared, "When a team of horses is working in unison, the load is much easier to pull. When not working together, the load is harder to pull. Just as in life, any team or relationship is rewarded with efficient teamwork."

But with increased mechanization in the early twentieth century, the country had little use for these work horses going forward. Many were sold to slaughterhouses, bringing the populations to a steady decline. Only the Amish, Mennonites, and other farmers (who utilize horse-drawn power) have kept the work-horses in full-time work mode. Luckily there are also some dedicated teamsters who have kept the draft horse hitches alive—sharing their love of the draft horses in our modern times.

And what about those Budweiser Clydesdale horses seen on television? The Clydesdales have been instrumental in creating a brand that gets the general public feverish about seeing a team of big draft horses. With their extraordinary grace, mixed with power and strength, the Budweiser Clydesdales have kept the vision of the draft horses alive and well in today's world. As a side note, at the Draft Horse Classic, the winning hitch takes a victory lap around

Father and son sharing a moment in the farm wagon class.

Six-up Action: All six heads lined up.

This stunning two-board grain wagon in the Farm Class is from the early 1900s.

This team of Belgian horses captivates the crowd in the log-skidding event.

The Carlaw Clydesdales—from British Columbia, Canada—on the rail in front of the grandstand.

the arena to the Budweiser Clydesdales' theme song—"Here Comes the King"—paying homage to these beloved horses.

We all have to admit that we love the exhilaration of watching the six-horse hitches. It's hard not to get excited when these big teams, adorned with their patent leather and brilliant chrome, come through the fairgrounds getting ready for the line-up. Make sure to put the Draft Horse Classic on your calendar for a guaranteed fun-filled weekend.

JUDGING DRAFT HORSE HITCHES

When watching these graceful gentle giants trot around the arena, the crowd reacts wildly to the energy and power each team exhibits. But the judges at these events have expert eyes and are looking for more than just flashiness. The crowd can easily pick out a team with good overall presentation: are the horses high-headed, do they have good conformation, do they cover the ground fluidly, and are they simply a beautiful team to watch?

But getting beyond the overall presentation, the judges are trained to look for other subtle differences, such as:

- Are the individual horses working correctly with their head forward and square in the traces or tugs?
- Does the team work well as a team—are the horses uniform in stride and in step, pulling equally, with taut traces or tugs?
- Does the team have consistent height and color?
- Are the horses well-groomed?
- Is the harness clean and in good condition?
- Does the harness fit properly and is it adjusted properly?

It is these subtle differences that distinguish the teams from one another. If all things are equal among two teams, then the fancy patent leather harnesses and chrome bling can break a tie.

The hitches are initially judged in preliminary heats, and then the highest-ranked teams will be brought back for the final heat and

A lady teamster in the Tandem Class.

Dancing Legs with Flying Feather.

A Percheron horse warming up for the Men's Pleasure Class.

placement. All of the hitches will make a few laps around the arena, usually starting in the counter-clockwise direction and then asked to reverse the direction so the judges can see the other side of the hitch. The draft horses will be judged in how they reverse directions under the skilled hands of the teamster.

Additionally, the judges will ask the draft horses to show at a trot and a walk. Finally, all the hitches will line up in the arena, at a complete stop, with all the teams facing the same direction. Each hitch is judged individually and each team is asked to back up a few steps.

With some practice of watching the draft horses, one can develop a keen eye for these subtleties. As for myself, I am always looking for that team with their heads held high, in unison, and stepping high…making my heart skip a beat!

The Rees Family Belgians—from Elk, Washington—coming into the corner.

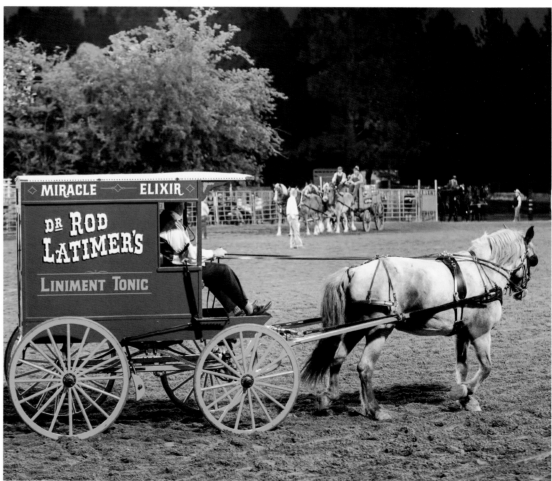

An authentically restored Snake Oil wagon in the Americana Class.

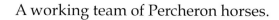

A working team of Percheron horses.

The California Cowgirls Equestrian Drill Team is a crowd favorite at the Draft Horse Classic. Nationally recognized for their breathtaking, high-speed maneuvers, the team performs at many rodeos, parades, and special events throughout California and Nevada. In this photo, a mother-daughter team is working together in the foreground.

A rider traversing the iconic Cougar Rock—a large volcanic outcropping that has been successfully crossed by thousands of horses. *Photo Credit: Bill Gore @ Gore / Baylor Photography.*

CHAPTER TWENTY

THE TEVIS CUP

While most people are asleep, in the dark hours before the sun rises, you will find a few hundred riders and horses nervously lining up in the chilly, morning air of the Sierra Nevada. Donning a layer of warm clothes, these riders are anxiously waiting for the start of one of the toughest races in the world of endurance riding—the Tevis Cup Ride, also known as the Western States Trail Ride. The ride has been held annually since 1955 and is administered by the Western States Trail Foundation. *Time* magazine named it a Top Ten Toughest Endurance Event in 2010, holding that honor alongside the Tour de France and the Iditarod Dog Sled Race.[66]

The Tevis Cup is a one-hundred-mile point-to-point endurance ride that crosses the Sierra Nevada—starting at an elevation of 7,200 feet, climbing up to 8,700 feet, and finally finishing in Auburn at an elevation of 1,200 feet. The ride follows old historic routes used by the Paiute and Washoe Indians, gold rush explorers, mule trains, wagon teams, and stagecoaches.

To earn a *Tevis Cup 100-Mile One-Day Western States Trail Ride* buckle, the horse and rider must complete the one-hundred miles within twenty-four hours while facing numerous challenges along the grueling route. Most years only about half of the riders finish the ride successfully. Buckle winners have ranged in age from 11 to 80 years old. Many breeds of horses have completed the Tevis Ride, but statistically Arabian horses have been the most successful overcoming the challenges of the course. Saddle mules have also participated in the Tevis Cup over the years. In 1974, a 9-year-old mule ridden by Eva Taylor won the Haggin Cup award, given to the equine judged to be in the most superior condition after the completion of the ride.

The ride officially begins at 5:15 am, usually in frosty temperatures, with approximately two hundred horses and mules riding in line on a single-track trail, trying to gain position in the early twilight hour. The Western States Trail is notoriously known for its precarious and steep sections. The ride includes Pucker Point—a breathtaking and gut-wrenching section of the trail which is very narrow on top of rocky cliffs above the American River, thousands of feet below. Riders also have to be able to cope with crossing a fifty-foot swinging bridge, witnessing nearby rattlesnakes on the trail, enduring 100° to 110°F temperatures, and finishing the ride in the dark. It is advised that the riders pre-ride the trail to become better acquainted with the route, especially in the dark sections.

The ride has been rescheduled or rerouted a few times due to heavy snowpack left over from the previous winter. The heavy snow causes rivers and creeks to be higher than usual and can create some challenging water and mud crossings. The ride has also been rescheduled due to wildfires—another force of nature to reckon with going forward.

Since the Sierra Nevada can be quite rugged, in addition to Mother Nature creating havoc along the course, riders need to be prepared for the many challenges. Parts of the course follow the footsteps of the early pioneers who succumbed to their deaths trying to cross the mighty Sierra Nevada.

Because the ride has many obstacles and unpredictable challenges, the Tevis Cup is committed to the humane treatment of all equines competing in the ride. The ride has numerous, mandatory veterinary checkpoints throughout the course. James Kerr, a DVM from Petaluma, who was the head veterinarian of the Tevis Cup from

A veterinarian is performing a pre-ride Vet Check of a horse. Along the Tevis Cup route, there are fourteen Vet Checks to ensure the safety and well-being of the horses and mules. Top-ten finishers are also randomly drug-tested to keep the Tevis Cup a drug-free sport—the welfare of the animals is their top priority. *Photo Credit: Bill Gore @ Gore / Baylor Photography.*

Frank Smith, his son, and good friend, Shane, trained and finished the Tevis Cup together in 2018. Frank says that most of their training was done in the backcountry—a lot of pack trips and trail riding. They also did a couple of shorter endurance rides (fifty miles) leading up to the Tevis Cup. Working at a pack station years ago, Frank learned firsthand how backcountry-packing was excellent conditioning for endurance rides. *Photo Credit: Bill Gore @ Gore / Baylor Photography.*

2000 to 2004, shared that the checkpoints involve monitoring for lameness, heart rate, and metabolic issues. Kerr has a keen insight into the demands of the ride since he earned a buckle in 2005. In addition to the checkpoints along the route, there is a post-race examination. The horse cannot be lame and the horse's heart rate cannot be more than sixty-eight beats per minute to achieve a finish.

Another feature of the ride, as a commitment to the welfare and proper conditioning of the equines, is the Haggin Cup Award—given to one of the top ten finishers the morning after the ride. The award is given to the horse or mule in the most superior condition after the ride. It is believed that the practice of selecting a *Best Condition* horse began when commanding officers in the US Cavalry would select a superior mount from their regiment to ride the day after arriving at their destination.[67]

Over the years, there have been numerous stories and encounters along the Western States Trail. Shannon Constanti from Auburn, California shared her memories from the nighttime portion of the trail ride with her horse, Om El Bernini Dream (Dreamcatcher SMF x Om El Benedict).

"The Western States Trail is one of the most majestic and breathtaking trails of its kind. There are so many sections of this trail that are inspiring and poignant beyond imagination. But for me, with no uncertainty, the most euphoric section of the Western States Trail has always been on the narrow, cliff-side trail above the American River in the vast darkness of nightfall—when both horse and rider are becoming fatigued—approximately fifteen miles from the finish line.

"The ability to relinquish control to your equine partner and experience them moving bravely with purpose into the dark unknown at a very forward pace, provides a bonding experience beyond measure. The sense of trust that you establish with your horse as they safely carry you down the trail, only relying on each other's instincts, is incomparable.

"We arrived at the American River Crossing around midnight, about twenty hours on the trail. I had pre-ridden the river many times in daylight so I would know the best path to cross in the darkness, as it is about a fifty-foot crossing, with many challenges if you don't cross with a plan. To my surprise, the river was much deeper at night than during the day due to the controlled release of the flow. But Bernini confidently entered the deep, cold, rushing water, and very quickly I realized that my feet, then my knees, and almost up to my hips were underwater. We emerged on the other side quite cold and wet. But Bernini knew he was nearing the finish line, as

he was well-versed on this section of trail and knew that his blanket, water, carrots, and hay would be waiting. We had conditioned on this section of trail hundreds of times and Bernini finished with stellar vet scores at completion," Constanti said of the nighttime ride.

Another rider, Crockett Dumas, a top-ten finisher from Escalante, Utah, shared one of his encounters along the trail. "I was jingling along at a good clip down the trail toward Kaput Spring on my horse, OT Gunplay RSI. This section of narrow, single-track trail has good footing and a gentle slope where good time can be made. Above the trail, the forest and understory are more open than most canyon slopes, so the visibility was about two hundred feet. Below the trail, the slope is a steep cliff—a place that is not forgiving to riders and horses who have disappeared over the edge. I was feeling elated as I was cruising along unabated, confident, and happy. Then suddenly out of the corner of my eye, a large bear came galloping towards us on a collision course with us. And I am thinking…'not good'!!"

"The bear did not let up nor did Gunplay. I kept thinking – 'this is not gonna end well.' At the point of collision, the trail clung to a thirty-six-inch old-growth Douglas fir tree. The bear crossed the trail right in front of Gunplay's nose while never breaking stride, darting up the tree. I goosed the bear's rear-end with my right hand as we passed by to keep him going up at a good rate.

"As Gunplay and I passed the tree, my thoughts started to recall all those people and horses that had gone over the edge at this location. With a few extra deep breaths, I calmed down, keeping focused on the trail ahead. While we headed up towards Michigan Bluff, I was feeling ecstatic—on cloud nine. And then a gray squirrel pops out on the trail three hundred feet away. Gunplay freaked out and reversed his direction, heading back toward the bear, leaving me hanging onto his ears and damn near unloaded me!

"This left me thinking—I was raised around black bears in the Great Smokies and became the first NPS mounted backcountry ranger at Glacier National Park in 1967, educating visitors on how to avoid grizzly bear confrontations. Gunplay was born and raised in the Sangre de Cristo Mountains of northern New Mexico where he had frequent bear encounters…but Gunplay had never seen a California gray squirrel!" Dumas shared.

With horses and mules, we can train and desensitize them for many situations—crossing bridges, oncoming cars, blowing flags, balloons, barking dogs, etc., but it's that unexpected potato chip bag or gray squirrel that gets us every time.

Moving the horses and mules to the pack station from the winter pastures.

CHAPTER TWENTY-ONE

HORSE & MULE DRIVES IN THE EASTERN SIERRA

A cloud of dust kicked up by hundreds of hooves with a few directive shouts from the cowboys—an annual ritual in the Eastern Sierra that reminds the locals that the packing season is about to begin. Every spring, a few of the packing outfits move their horses and mules from their winter grounds, in the Owens Valley, to the pack stations located at higher elevations, near the high country.

Fifty years ago, most of the pack stations moved their livestock on the trails from the winter pastures as a necessity. With the advent of modern livestock trailers, only Frontier Pack Train, Mammoth Lakes Pack Outfit, and Rock Creek Pack Station continue this tradition every spring and fall in present times. The clients that attend these drives are a part of the working crew helping to move the livestock on old trails and roads used by past generations. These trail drives can last anywhere from three to five days but create memories that last a lifetime.

Faster-paced than a cattle drive, these horse drives are a fun way to step back in time and spend a few days on the western range. There's no shortage of spectacular views of the Sierra Nevada on these drives—it's a great way to refresh your soul and ponder some of life's mysteries.

While the guests indulge in a hearty breakfast, the wranglers start early in the morning, rounding up and saddling the riding stock. Most of the horses and mules have made this trip many times prior, so they know the routine and look forward to their days in the backcountry.

"Too often I would hear men boast of the miles covered that day, rarely of what they had seen." —Louis L'Amour

But sometimes the mules know the routine all too well. One year, on the last day of the spring Frontier Horse Drive, the mules were approaching Silver Lake (en route to the pack station), and the cold water looked very inviting. After putting in many miles that day, a few of the mules made a beeline for the water. Jumping off a small ledge, they made a big-splash entry—like a kid performing a cannonball-maneuver into the pool. But not far away, there was a wedding ceremony taking place, and the mules took center stage. I'm sure the bride and groom still talk about their unexpected guests crashing their party that day!

Dramatic silhouettes captured on the horse drive in Owens Valley.

Faster-paced than a cattle drive, these horse drives are a fun way to step back in time and spend a few days on the western range.

Keeping an eye on the herd as it moves to summer grounds.

"Twenty years from now, you will be more disappointed by the things you didn't do than by the ones you did do."

—Mark Twain

185

Moving one hundred head of horses and mules on the annual Frontier Pack Train Horse Drive.

There is never a shortage of great views while moving horses and mules on the annual Frontier Pack Train Horse Drive.

The Horse Drive

My pardner will shurnuff earn his keep today, tomorrow, and the next
Grass hay breakfast will wear off, this day will get longish soon—
Daybreak was but a glow on the jagged Sierra horizon

When the wrangler opened the gate, the mules blew through
At a long high trot, chargin' at about six abreast at first
The horses were fresh and antsy, rearin' to get going
Spent the first few miles tryin' to hold 'em back
And by the time the sun touched 'em, they were stringing out

There is the pungent odor of freshly-crushed sage by hardened hooves
One-hundred times four, a smell so strong you can taste it
Stifling a swallow, sometimes burning inside my nose, a natural high
There's a rhythmic melodious plod as the mules single-file through the high desert
Like box-cars on a train, so evenly spaced, their shadows strung together
On the sand, in a syncopated line in time

Last day of the drive, the earliest start, weary, footsore and bone tired
The sunrise not even a glow, tempts imagination and longing
A flood of mixed, contrary emotions hit hard
On the one hand, the finality of an annual job
On the other, the end of bygone days – an Old West experience.

© Sallie Knowles Joseph

In a chaotic fire situation, horses are often difficult to load into trailers and may flee, or even run into the fire.
Photo Credit: © Gene Blevins, Zuma Press.

CHAPTER TWENTY-TWO

BEHIND THE FIRELINE AT THE CAMP FIRE: RESCUING ANIMALS AND LIVESTOCK

The fire started near the community of Concow, California early on the morning of November 8, 2018. By 8 a.m., the Butte County Sheriff's Department issued an evacuation order for the nearby town of Paradise. During the next hour, the fire approached Paradise and the town became dark with ash falling everywhere. As the Diablo winds picked up speed (a hot, dry, easterly wind that comes down from the Sierra Nevada in the fall), the fire became ferocious, burning everything in its path. Some did not have time to evacuate and left their homes in slippers. Others were at work and could not return home to evacuate their animals.

The Camp Fire sadly became the most destructive wildfire in California's history, burning more than 18,000 structures and causing at least eighty-four fatalities. It was especially hard on the pets and livestock in the area. Some people wrongly put guilt on the horse-owners who left their horses behind—but for many, there were literally only seconds to evacuate…or rather run.

The North Valley Animal Disaster Group (NVADG) was the first group called in to assist the Butte County Animal Control (the lead agency). NVADG is a group of dedicated volunteers that partner with emergency services in disaster situations. The volunteers train year-round on fireline safety, radio communication, emergency equipment, animal rescue, and animal handling—always on call and ready to respond. Their training became a huge asset in this tragic disaster unfolding throughout the day of November 8.

NVADG set up phone lines and deployed teams behind the fire lines following the evacuation orders. Norm Rosene, the vice president and public information officer for the NVADG, shared with me, "Our mission was to evacuate and shelter animals. So while setting up evacuation teams, we began to set up three emergency animal shelters—with a large animal shelter set up at a nearby fairground. We were involved with animal evacuation and sheltering for a week after the evacuation orders were lifted and also involved with emergency animal shelters into the month of January 2019."

There were many horrific images being broadcast on television and the internet of the fire's damage. Horses and donkeys were seen running loose, trying to find a safe haven. The firefighters, emergency crews, and volunteers were working countless hours with no end in sight.

Rosene shared, "We were working fourteen- to sixteen-hour shifts during the first week. It was a huge fire and the workload was tremendous. As time progressed, other aid teams came to assist: International Fund for Animal Welfare (IFAW), Red Rover, American Humane, The Humane Society of the United States, ASPCA, USDA, Cowboy 911, the National Guard, and others. In 2015, I was in Nepal responding to the earthquake, but the destruction of this fire was far greater. During the worst of the fire, the winds were blowing 40-50 mph and the fire reacted like a horizontal blow torch. I heard the fire 'consumed an acre per second.' It incinerated cars and melted metal like it was wax.

"Our evacuation teams rescued hundreds of animals including livestock and moved many of them to the emergency animal shelters. Many livestock animals were left behind during the fire since the owners only had seconds to evacuate. Additionally, thousands of animals were fed and watered in place behind the evacuation lines

until the area was safe enough for the owners to return. Some days, we distributed twenty tons of feed and animal food to the shelters and supply depots. We also fed and watered cattle and hundreds of beehives—an exhaustive day's work."

Many animal owners were able to reunite with their animals, and the heroic efforts of the emergency crews and volunteer groups should be applauded. They are the unsung heroes who are always on call—at a moment's notice.

HOW TO BE PREPARED FOR A FIRE EVACUATION WITH YOUR EQUINE

Each horse, mule, or donkey should be permanently identified with a brand, microchip, tattoo, or photograph. Keep a set of records with you that includes the animal's age, sex, breed, and color.

Keep halters ready for your equine. On each halter attach a luggage tag with pertinent information and contact numbers.

In a watertight envelope, keep a set of your equine's Coggins tests, vet papers, and vital medical history/needs, allergies, emergency contacts, and identification photographs. Store them in a safe place but accessible during an emergency.

Make sure your equine is accustomed to being loaded in a trailer—this is the most important factor when evacuating equine. Know where to take your animals in an evacuation. If possible, make arrangements with another equine owner in a nearby region out of harm's way.

Top left: During fires, having trained and well-equipped animal rescuers allows for safe evacuation from the fire zone. *Photo Credit: © Paul Kitagaki, Sacramento Bee/Zuma Press.*

Botto left: NVADG volunteer sheltering a horse in place behind the evacuation during the deadly 2018 Camp Fire. *Photo courtesy of Janice Rosene.*

Rescuing animals during a fire can be a bit chaotic, but the volunteers of NVADG are trained and equipped to work in such conditions. *Photo courtesy of Melody Herman.*

Make sure you have adequate fuel in all vehicles during the fire season. Trailers should be backed into a position that is easy to access and hook-up quickly.

Have a back-up plan in case Plan A is not possible. Share your evacuation plans with friends and neighbors.

When disaster strikes, don't wait until the last minute to evacuate. Don't leave your equine behind, if the situation is safe for both of you to leave.

Have supplies ready—water, feed, medications for several days.

For more information, please visit the Humane Society's website, https://www.humanesociety.org/resources/disaster-preparedness-horses, or North Valley Animal Disaster Group's website.

Backcountry Horsemen of California (BCHC) members haul tools into the backcountry for trail repair. After a wet and/or snowy winter, trails have extensive damage from water runoff and downed trees. The dedication of the BCHC to ongoing trail repair benefits all who use the trails.

CHAPTER TWENTY-THREE

BACKCOUNTRY HORSEMEN OF CALIFORNIA

In 1981, a group of private and commercial packers formed the High Sierra Stock Users Association as a means to represent horsemen in dealing with the administration of public lands. Five years later, the group changed its name to Backcountry Horsemen of California (BCHC) and joined with Montana, Idaho, and Washington to form the national group—Back Country Horsemen of America. This national group is committed to protecting the access of equestrians to public lands, assisting with trail maintenance, and keeping trails clear for all user groups.

The BCHC provides safety training for backcountry packing, chainsaw training, and a variety of other educational programs. In addition, the group has an annual gathering—called the Rendezvous—held in different locations to provide hands-on equine training, horse and mule packing seminars, and a variety of entertaining venues.

The BCHC partnered with the Leave No Trace Center for Outdoor Ethics, a non-profit organization formed to educate the public about their recreational impact on nature, in 2011. The BCHC shares the principles with their group members and the public:

1. Plan ahead and prepare
2. Travel and camp on durable surfaces
3. Dispose of waste properly
4. Leave what you find
5. Minimize campfire impacts
6. Respect wildlife
7. Be considerate of other visitors

The BCHC has worked with other organizations helping to clear trails, benefiting all who use the backcountry trails. Members provide stock, trail tools, and manpower to help with the backlog of trail maintenance on hundreds of miles of trail in California.

Lloyd Erlandson, 2019 BCHC President, shared his thoughts about the ongoing efforts of the BCHC: "BCHC members try to stay current on issues of importance to all equestrian trail users. Front country or backcountry use is important to all. We maintain an ongoing relationship with each of the different public land agencies and supply input when appropriate. Many hours are spent volunteering in the backcountry working on trails and going to meetings to be a voice for all horse people."

TIPS FOR HIKING ON TRAILS WITH HORSES OR MULES

- When you meet a horse or mule on the trail, step off the trail on the downhill slope. This makes you appear less threatening.
- Greet the rider and ask if you are okay where you are. Your voice will help alert the animal that you're human.
- If you're hiking with a dog, keep it firmly heeled, and let the rider know if your dog is likely to bark.
- Remain visible to the animal.
- Stand quietly as the horses or mules pass.

BCHC volunteer service projects not only require packing in necessary tools and equipment but also packing in essential provisions and supplies to keep trail maintenance workers fed, clothed, and sheltered. *Photo Credit: Michael W. King.*

BCHC members haul tools and gear into the backcountry for trail repair. Members help maintain trails throughout the state, benefiting all that use the trails. *Photo Credit: Michael W. King.*

A tremendous amount of planning is required for backcountry projects. To reach this trail-blocking 66-inch diameter Jeffrey pine, a volunteer crew traveled eight miles one-way on a trail that climbed 4,000 feet in elevation. In addition to food and equipment for their overnight stay, the crew packed in a 60-pound griphoist that provided 16,000 pounds of pull to move the cut tree-section from the trail. *Photo Credit: Bill Carter.*

Sometimes you have to grab life by the reins and live life to the fullest. Don't make excuses…even a wagon accident shouldn't slow you down. I want to thank all my amazing friends who helped me recover from my accident and in turn, finish the book. Your dedication to the western lifestyle inspires me every day and I dedicate this book to you!

For print inquiries, please visit www.sandypowellphoto.com

Endnotes

Chapter One: The Discovery of California's Gold

1. Wikipedia, "History of California," last modified March 21, 2019, https://en.wikipedia.org/wiki/History_of_California

2. Six Incredible Sierra Nevada, California Snow Records, last modified November 25, 2014, https://snowbrains.com/six-incredible-sierra-nevada-ca-snow-records/

Chapter Two: The Journey to California by Wagon Train

3. Carlisle S. Abbott, *Recollections of a California Pioneer*, (New York, Neale Publishing Company, 1917), 65.

4. Doyce B. Nunis, Jr., *The Bidwell-Bartleson Party: 1841 California Emigrant Adventure*, (Santa Cruz, California, Western Tanager Press, 1992), 11.

5. George R. Stewart, *The California Trail*, (Lincoln, University of Nebraska Press, 1962), 57.

6. Stewart, *The California Trail*, 72.

7. George R. Stewart, *Ordeal by Hunger: The Story of the Donner Party*, Reprint of 1936 edition, (New York, Houghton Mifflin Company, 1988), 133.

8. Stewart, *The California Trail*, 231.

9. Abbott, *Recollections of a California Pioneer*, 27.

10. James Abbey, *California: A Trip Across the Plains in the Spring of 1850*, E-Book, Library of Congress, Reprinted in 1933, (New Albany, Indiana, Norman and Nunemacher, 1850).

11. Abbey, *California: A Trip Across the Plains*.

12. Abbey, *California: A Trip Across the Plains*.

13. National Oregon/California Trail Center at Montpelier, Idaho, last updated 2019, https://oregontrailcenter.org/dangers

Chapter Three: The Overland Mail

14. *Bodie Standard*, September 18, 1878.

15. *Stagecoach West* Television Series, *The Bold Whip*, Season 1, Episode 33, 1961.

16. John Boessenecker, *When Law Was in the Holster: The Frontier Life of Bob Paul*, (Norman, Oklahoma, University of Oklahoma Press, 2012), p. 96-97.

17. Wikipedia, "1850 United States Census," last modified on March 8, 2019, https://en.wikipedia.org/wiki/1850_United_States_Census

18. Wikipedia, "1860 United States Census," last modified on March 8, 2019, https://en.wikipedia.org/wiki/1860_United_States_Census

19. Wikipedia, "Maritime History of California: Alta California Maritime Activities," last modified on March 3, 2019, https://en.wikipedia.org/wiki/Maritime_history_of_California

20. Carl H. Scheele, *A Short History of the Mail Service*, (City of Washington: Smithsonian Institution Press, 1970), 80-81.

21. Thomas H. Thompson and Albert West, *History of Nevada with Illustrations and Biographical Sketches of the Prominent Men and Pioneers*, (Berkeley: Howell-North Publishers, 1958), 102-105; and Hubert Howe Bancroft, *The Works of Hubert Howe Bancroft: History of Nevada, Colorado, and Wyoming*, Vol. XXV (San Francisco, The History Company Publishers, 1890), 226-227.

22. Ralph Moody, *Stagecoach West*, (Lincoln, University of Nebraska Press, 1967), 69.

23. Moody, *Stagecoach West*, 69.

24. Le Roy Hafen, *The Overland Mail, 1849-1869: Promotor of Settlements, Precursor of Railroads*, Reprint of 1926 Edition, (New York: AMS Press, Inc., 1969), 64-69.

25. Hafen, *The Overland Mail*, 95-99; Richard A. Bartlett, *The New Country: A Social History of the American Frontier, 1776-1890*, (New York, Oxford University Press, 1974), 302-303; and Frederic Paxson, *History of the American Frontier, 1763-1893*, (Cambridge, Massachusetts, The Riverside Press, 1924), 463-464.

26. Ormsby, Waterman L., *The Butterfield Overland Mail*, (San Marino, California, The Huntington Library, 1942), 91.

27. Edmund Hope Verney, *An Overland Journey from San Francisco to New York by Way of Salt Lake City*, (London, Good Words, 1865), 381-382.

28. Verney, *An Overland Journey from San Francisco to New York*, 383.

29. Mark Twain, e-book, Reprint of 1872 Edition, 2018.

30. Robert E. Pinkerton, *The First Overland Mail*, e-book, Papamoa Press, Reprint of 1953 Edition, 2017.

31. Alvin F. Harlow, *Old Waybills*, (New York, Appleton-Century Company, 1934), 206.

Chapter Four: The Pony Express

32. George A. Root and Russell K. Hickman, "Pike's Peak Express Companies, Part I: Solomon and Republican Route," *Kansas Historical Quarterly*, Vol. XII, No. 3 (August, 1944), 163-195.

33. Le Roy Hafen, *The Overland Mail, 1849-1869: Promotor of Settlements, Precursor of Railroads*, Reprint of 1926 Edition (New York: AMS Press, Inc., 1969), 150-153.

34. Alexander Majors, *Seventy Years on the Frontier: Alexander Major's Memoirs of a Lifetime on the Border (1893)*, edited by Colonel Prentiss Ingraham, Reprint, (Columbus, Ohio: Long's College Book Co., 1950), 184.

35. National Pony Express Association, 2019, https://nationalponyexpress.org/historic-pony-express-trail/

36. Hafen, *The Overland Mail, 1849-1869*, 179.

37. Ralph Moody, *Stagecoach West*, (Lincoln, University of Nebraska Press,1967), 183; and Majors, *Seventy Years on the Frontier*, 184-185.

38. *San Francisco Daily Evening Bulletin*, March 30, 1860; and Majors, *Seventy Years on the Frontier*, 175.

39. Gladys Shaw Erskine, *Broncho Charlie: A Saga of Saddle*, (New York: Thomas Y. Crowell Company, 1934), 30.

40. Majors, *Seventy Years on the Frontier*, 176.

41. Majors, *Seventy Years on the Frontier*, 176.

42. *Deseret News*, November 28, 1860.

43. *St. Louis Missouri Democrat*, January 21, 1861.

44. Raymond W. and Mary Lund Settle, *Saddles and Spurs: The Pony Express Saga*, (Harrisburg, Pennsylvania: The Stackpole Company, 1955), 196.

Chapter Six: Gunfighters and Vigilante Justice During the Gold Rush

45. John Boessenecker, *Gold Dust & Gunsmoke: Tales of Gold Rush Outlaws, Gunfighters, Lawmen and Vigilantes*, (New York, John Wiley & Sons, 1999), 297.

Chapter Seven: Bodie

46. *Bodie Standard*, September 18, 1878.

47. California Department of Parks and Recreation, 2019, https://www.parks.ca.gov/?page_id=21622

48. James Watson and Doug Brodie, *Big Bad Bodie: High Sierra Ghost Town*, e-book, Xlibris Corporation, 2000.

49. Riley Moffat, *Population History of Western U.S. Cities and Towns, 1850-1990*, (Lanham, Maryland, Scarecrow Press, Inc., 1996), 21.

Chapter Nine: Mule Packing in the Sierra Nevada

50. American Mule Museum, "History of the Mule," Last modified March, 2019, http://www.mulemuseum.org/history-of-the-mule.html

51. Brian Kalet, "California's Highest 100 Peaks," Last modified March 2019, https://www.summitpost.org/california-s-highest-100-peaks/373601

52. Louise A. Jackson, *The Mule Men: A History of Stock Packing in the Sierra Nevada*, (Missoula, Montana, Mountain Press Publishing Company, 2004), 88.

Chapter Ten: Basque Sheepherding in the Sierra Nevada

53. Donald A. Potter, *Forested Communities of the Upper Montane in the Central and Southern Sierra Nevada*, General Technical Report PSW-GTR-169, USDA Forest Service, Pacific Southwest Research Station, 1998, 36.

54. Stephen Bass and George Ansolabehere, *The Basques of Kern County*, (Bakersfield, California, Castle Printing Group, 2012), 161.

55. L.T. Burcham, *California Range Land, An Historico-Ecological Study of the Range Resource of California*, (Sacramento, California, Division of Forestry Department of Natural Resources, State of California, 1957), 255.

56. Stephen Bass and George Ansolabehere, *The Basques of Kern County*, 196.

57. L.T. Burcham, *California Range Land, An Historico-Ecological Study of the Range Resource of California*, 156.

Chapter Eleven: One Hundred Mules Walking the Los Angeles Aqueduct

58. Louis Sahagun, *The L.A. Aqueduct at 100*, L.A. Times, October 28, 2013, http://graphics.latimes.com/me-aqueduct/

59. Wikipedia, "Los Angeles Aqueduct," last modified June 27, 2020, https://en.wikipedia.org/wiki/Los_Angeles_Aqueduct

60. The Center for Land Use Interpretation, *Navigating on Owens Lake: A Brief History of Boating on Eastern Sierra's Inland Sea*, Winter Newsletter, 2015, http://www.clui.org/newsletter/winter-2015/navigating-owens-lake

Chapter Twelve: USFS Pack Mules

61. Wilderness Connect, Wilderness Statistics Reports, Last modified April 1, 2019, https://www.wilderness.net/NWPS/chartResults?chartType=AcreageByStateMost

Chapter Seventeen: Twenty Mule Team

62. Harold O. Wright, *20 Mule Team Days in Death Valley*, (Twentynine Palms, California, Calico Press, 1955), 12.

63. Wikipedia, "Twenty-mule team," Last modified December 10, 2018, https://en.wikipedia.org/wiki/Twenty-mule_team

64. John Randolph Spears, *Illustrated Sketches of Death Valley and Other Borax Deserts of the Pacific Coast*, (New York, McNally & Company, 1892), 99-101.

65. Spears, *Illustrated Sketches of Death Valley*, 98.

Chapter Twenty: The Tevis Cup

66. *Time* Magazine, Gilbert Cruz, 2010 http://content.time.com/time/specials/packages/article/0,28804,1869820_1869688_1869685,00.html

67. Wikipedia, "Tevis Cup", last modified on January 21, 2019, https://en.wikipedia.org/wiki/Tevis_Cup